Classic Cloth DOLLS

BEAUTIFUL
FABRIC DOLLS AND
CLOTHES FROM THE
VOGUE® PATTERNS
COLLECTION

Linda Carr

Classic Cloth DOLLS

BEAUTIFUL
FABRIC DOLLS AND
CLOTHES FROM THE
VOGUE® PATTERNS
COLLECTION

Linda
Carr

sixth&springbooks

Sixth&Spring Books
233 Spring Street
New York, New York 10013

Editorial Director
Trisha Malcolm

Art Director
Ben Ostasiewski

Managing Editor
Annemarie McNamara

Writer
Beth Baumgartel

Associate Editor
Jean Guirguis

Graphic Designers
Lila Chin
Anna Bolton
Denise D'Abramo

Production Managers
David Joinnides
Lillian Esposito

Book Concept
Caroline Politi

Promotions Manager
Theresa McKeon

**Publisher and President,
Sixth&Spring Books**
Art Joinnides

Manufactured in China

1 3 5 7 9 10 8 6 4 2

Library of Congress Cataloging-in-Publication Data

Carr, Linda, 1943-
    Classic cloth dolls: beautiful fabric dolls from the Vogue patterns collection / by Linda Carr.
        p. cm.
    ISBN 1-931543-04-6 Trade
    ISBN 1-931543-49-6 Paper
    1. Dollmaking. 2. Cloth dolls. 3. Doll clothes. I. Title.

TT175.C33 2001
745.592'21—dc21   2001020653

LINDA CARR DOLLS

Introduction

The Linda Carr line of fabric dolls all started with Linda's simple desire to find a beautiful cloth doll for her daughter. Being unsuccessful in her search, she decided to create the doll herself. Armed with an art school degree, several years of experience as an art teacher, and a love of fabric, the adventure began.

Linda's first dolls were never planned, they just happened as she stitched and manipulated cotton gauze fabric into soft sculptured faces. The more dolls she made, the more inspired she became. Soon, Linda was exhibiting her doll collection at craft fairs—and they caused a stir of excitement. She began fielding far-reaching requests for her uniquely charming dolls. The dolls quickly led to stuffed animals and other toys—and the Linda Carr home-based cottage industry was born!

By this time Linda was a full-time mother of two by day and a successful doll designer by night—and her business was continuing to grow. She took on a staff of five women to help sew and stuff her dolls and toys, while she continued to stitch all the faces and do all the designing herself.

Well into her tenth year as an entrepreneur, Linda donated a doll to a fund-raising event. The doll caught the eye of the Vice President of Merchandising at Vogue Patterns, who offered Linda the opportunity to share her beautiful designs with home sewers. By this time, Linda's business had grown so much that she was finding it increasingly difficult to produce one-of-a-kind items to meet the demand. Fortunately, by designing patterns, Linda was offered the opportunity to reach a whole new audience of customers and eliminate the worry of unfulfilled orders. And so began a long-term relationship between Linda Carr and Vogue Craft that continues to this day.

In the twenty years since Linda created her first doll for Vogue, she has designed and produced hundreds of keepsake quality dolls, accessories, and stuffed toys, each more charming than the next! With the introduction and tremendous popularity of 18" (46cm) dolls, Linda thought it time to add her own 18" (46cm) doll to the line. The first doll, called Amanda, sold so well that a "family" of dolls was added, as well as clothes and accessories.

Linda strongly feels that her doll designs must be easy to sew. She loves making dolls today as much as she did those many years ago when her two-year-old daughter provided the inspiration. She claims that dollmaking is her favorite creative medium, as it enables her to combine her art school training with her love for sewing and fabrics. With this book, Linda shares her talents, skills, knowledge, and experience with home sewers to enable them to create their own Linda Carr designed fabric dolls and wardrobes. Beautiful step-by-step photographs clearly illustrate every detail in the creative process, from sewing and stuffing the doll, to painting its face and making its wardrobe. All of the pattern pieces are included along with a comprehensive list of fabric and notion requirements. Enter the world of dollmaking…it's a wonderful place to be!

Table of Contents

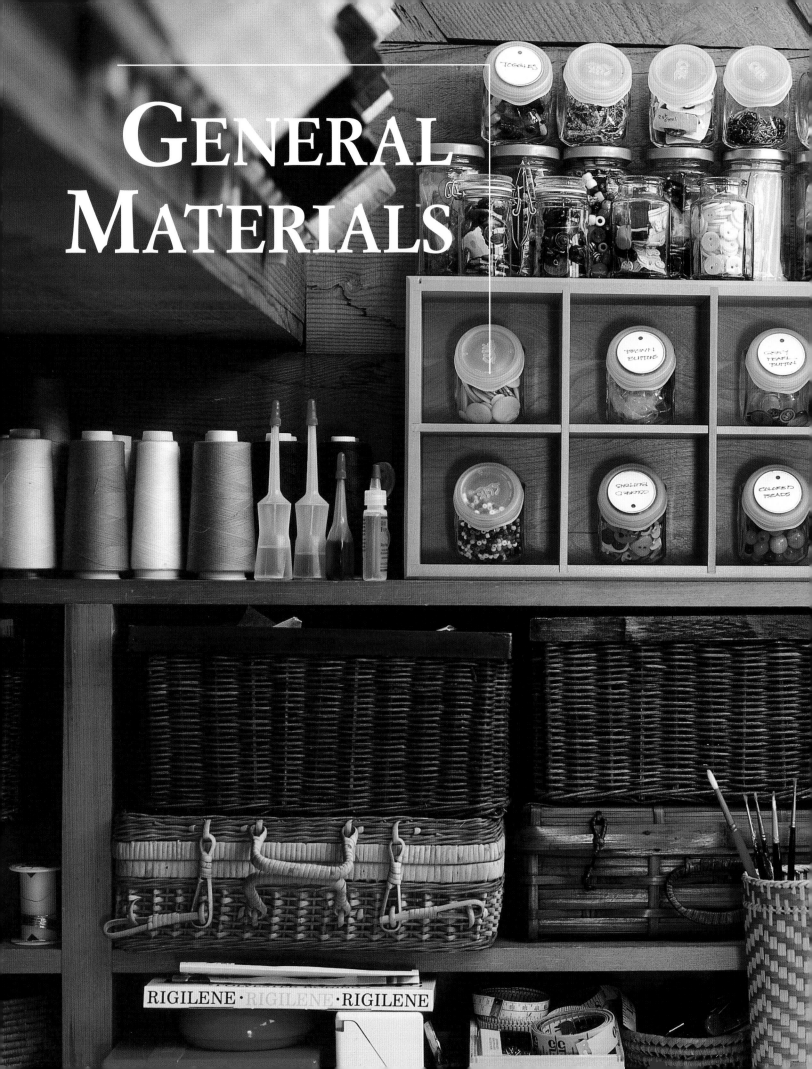

GENERAL
MATERIALS

CHAPTER

1

EXPLORE THE MANY PLEASURES of fabric dollmaking…it's easy, inexpensive, and very rewarding! Sewing, stuffing, painting the face, and dressing the doll are within the realm of even the most novice sewer and decorative painter. And only a minimal investment in tools and materials is required. In fact, a beautiful doll with a modest wardrobe can often be made from bits and scraps of material found around the home! All of the necessary fabrics, notions, and supplies are available through traditional retail and mail order outlets. For additional shopping information, refer to the resource list on page 158.

Keep in mind that dolls made for children should adhere to safety regulations. Work with low flammability fabrics and nontoxic paints. Make sure seams are securely stitched so they do not open. Choose buttons, beads, and other small parts and accessories that are large enough to prohibit choking, or eliminate them completely if the child is under the age of five.

This doll benefits from a combination of knit and woven fabrics. Woven fabric is used for the body of the doll, where dimension is created through pattern shape, darts, and curves. A stable knit is used for the face of the doll to help emulate the soft sculptured look of a real person.

Fabric

DOLL BODY

The body of the doll, including the back of the head, requires medium-weight, tightly-woven broadcloth, linen, muslin, or duck cloth. Closely-woven fabrics do not ravel as easily as other fabrics, which is important when sewing the smaller seam allowances used on doll patterns. Heavyweight fabrics are too bulky, and lightweight fabrics do not have enough body to support the structure of the doll. Minimally textured fabric is suitable, as long as it does not distract from the doll's important details.

The color of the body fabric is a matter of personal choice; however, soft pinks, peaches, and browns are always appropriate (a peachy middle tone is a good choice). The color of the fabric does appear lighter once there is stuffing or interfacing behind it. Position a piece of white paper behind the fabric you are considering to get a sense of how it will look once it has been interfaced, sewn, and stuffed.

Buy the best-quality fabric you can afford, since the quality of the body fabric largely determines the quality of the doll.

DOLL FACE

The most suitable fabric for the doll's face is stable, polyester knit. Because the back of the head is made from woven cloth, it remains firm, while the knit face stretches slightly to acquire the shape and contour of the facial features created by the fiberfill stuffing. Knit fabric also accepts makeup better than woven, and the soft texture of the knit is a perfect background for the natural look of makeup.

Try to match the color of the knit fabric as closely as possible to the color of the woven fabric; however, a slightly yellow cast or undertone does help the makeup stand out better. If the two fabrics don't match perfectly, use face makeup to naturally blend the colors together at the neck area.

If you can't find the color fabric you want for your doll, dye unbleached muslin and/or the stable knit to create any variety of skin tones, including African-American and ethnic subtleties. It's usually easy enough to find appropriate body fabric; however, it is sometimes necessary to dye the face fabric to get the desired flesh tone.

If you prefer not to dye fabric for the face, use the body fabric, but cut it on the bias grainline, so it stretches slightly.

HOW TO DYE FABRIC FOR THE FACE & BODY

Mix the purchased dye and hot water together in a basin until the dye dissolves. Submerge the fabric in the dye bath completely. Stir the water and fabric occasionally, checking the color every few minutes. Soak the fabric until it is slightly darker than the desired shade, as fabric tends to lighten as it dries (and you can always dye it again to make it darker). When the fabric reaches the desired color, remove it from the dye bath, and squeeze out all the excess water. Rinse the fabric in cool water and place it in the dryer or press it while it's still damp to heat-set the color.

For an aged look, dye unbleached muslin in tea: Brew a quart (1 liter) of very strong tea with eight or nine tea bags. Stir the mixture occasionally while it brews so that the color is even. Remove the bags and soak the fabric in the tea until it is slightly darker than the desired shade (fabric lightens as it dries). Place the fabric in a dryer or press it while it's still damp to set the color.

TIP: *Use a middle tone dye; you can always add more color. Remove the fabric early if the color is too dark.*

INTERFACING

For fabric stability and to eliminate the possibility of visible seam allowances on the right side of the doll, apply lightweight, fusible tricot to the body and face fabric. Stabilizing the fabric also makes it easier to sew around the curves of the hands and feet. Tricot is the best choice—other interfacings are too stiff. It's easiest to apply the tricot to the fabric prior to cutting out the pattern pieces.

DOLL CLOTHING

Doll clothing is small, so work with the best, most luxurious fabric you can afford. Fine cottons, elegant tapestries, and sumptuous silks tend to be cost prohibitive when sewing home furnishings or adult clothing, so treat yourself to the joy and pleasure of working with these top-quality fabrics when you sew doll clothes and accessories.

Doll clothing is also a great way to recycle bits and pieces of fabric from old clothing or home linens. Flea markets, antique sales, and consignment shops provide a wealth of exquisite fabrics. Scale, color, and pattern are all a matter of personal taste—basically anything goes, as long as you love it.

Add beads, ruffles, bows, flowers, trims, and embroidery to give the clothing a sense of grandeur. To ensure that the trim matches the fabric in both color and scale, try making it yourself. Several suggestions for making fabulous-looking trim are included in chapter two.

Depending on your preference, you can make your own doll hair with yarn or thread, or choose from the large selection of beautiful doll wigs available (see resources, page 158).

Hair

If you prefer to make your own doll hair, worsted wool yarn is a good choice. It has a soft hand with natural and subtle-looking color variations. Rug yarn, curly mohair, boucle, chenille, and even cotton thread make interesting doll hair. For a truly natural look, hand dye natural yarns or combine light tones of similar yarns together to obtain the realistic shading of human hair.

There are many ways to draw or paint the facial features of a doll! Chapter four features clear and complete instructions and visuals on how to apply paints, pencils, and everyday makeup to create beautiful, lifelike doll faces. Note that as an alternative to painting, the facial features can be embroidered.

Pencils, Paint & Makeup

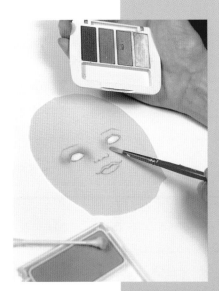

Colored Pencils are easy to control, making them ideal for both outlining and filling in the details of the facial features. They create drama with their luminous color and add natural-looking shading to the face. A selection of five or six colors is adequate: two shades of brown for outlining the eyes, lips, and nose; two shades of pink, coral, or peach for the lips; and a canary yellow for the eyes. (Light blue/green and amber are good alternatives to yellow.) PrismaColor® Pencils are used throughout chapter four and specific color references are listed in the materials section.

Everyday Makeup is used to give the face a natural look. Powder blush and eye shadow are great for shading, blending, highlighting, and creating a soft appearance. Two shades of pink or coral powder blush, one slightly brighter than the other, are used repeatedly to blend and soften the facial features. A neutral, beige eye shadow is also instrumental in creating the soft glow that radiates from this doll. When working with makeup, start with a light application and build up by adding layers of color. Keep in mind that once the color is applied to the fabric it can be close to impossible to get off.

Acrylic Paint is used to give depth to the pupils of the eyes. Black and white paints are the only colors needed.

Application Tools vary with each step. Have several new paintbrushes on hand in sizes #2, #4, and #7 to apply both paint and makeup. You will also need a medium-size makeup brush and a handful of cotton swabs. A pencil sharpener is handy to keep pencil points sharp.

Miscellaneous Supplies include dressmaker's carbon paper and a ballpoint pen to transfer the facial details to the fabric, and hair spray or clear acrylic spray to set the painted face. Fine-tip permanent markers are useful for outlining features, adding finishing touches, and rendering precise details, such as eyelashes. Try the markers on scrap fabric first to make sure the ink doesn't bleed. Never use felt-tip markers.

Standard, cotton-wrapped polyester thread is fine for
dollmaking. Try to match the thread as closely as possible to the fabric, particularly for the doll body, since
stitches are visible on tightly-stuffed sections. If you
can't find a perfect match, go a shade lighter rather than
darker. Use quilting thread or buttonhole twist to hand-sew the doll closed.

Thread

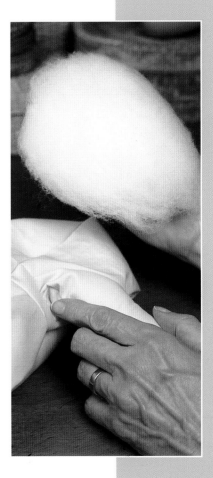

Polyester fiberfill is the stuffing of choice. In addition to being inexpensive, it's easy to handle, doesn't lump, washes and dry cleans well, and is nonallergenic. There are varying grades of fiberfill, some softer than others. For a smoother finish, work with the best-quality fiberfill. (Quality refers to weight and degree of bounce.) A dowel, blunt knitting needle, ruler, or stuffing tool is necessary to pack the fiberfill firmly into the body and head of the doll.

Stuffing

In addition to the supplies listed above, you will need: a sewing machine; an iron and ironing board; straight pins (fine silk pins are worth the investment); small scissors for clipping; large scissors for cutting; a disappearing ink pen; an iron and seam roll; spray adhesive; white cardboard or foam core (for the soles of the feet); and, paper-backed fusible web. Stuffing tools should be small and have a blunt end to avoid poking a hole through the fabric. Try a screwdriver, dowels of varying widths, hemostats, or even chopsticks. Use a pointed tool, such as a knitting needle, to push out corners or small-sculpted areas such as fingers.

Basic Sewing Tools

A doll-size sleeveboard makes ironing small doll clothes easier. Even a regular-size sleeveboard is more suitable than a standard ironing board for working with the small pieces involved in making dolls and their clothes.

Tools for Small-Scale Sewing

Dritz® for Dolls offers two padded doll-size dressforms, one for an 18" (46cm) doll, and the other for an 11½" (29.3cm) doll. Also from Dritz is a narrow, ⅜" (1cm)-wide tape measure that is easy to wrap around tiny waists and wrists. This new line of sewing notions is scaled down and includes over sixty-five unique items, such as miniature fasteners, mini shoulder pads, and even 1" (2.5cm) personality hearts for inside the doll body!

The Hockey Stick is a long, narrow metal tool with a flat end that helps guide and control small pieces of fabric under the presser foot. The Little Foot™ or any patchwork foot is designed to sew ¼" (6mm) seam allowances.

GENERAL INSTRUCTIONS & BASIC SKILLS

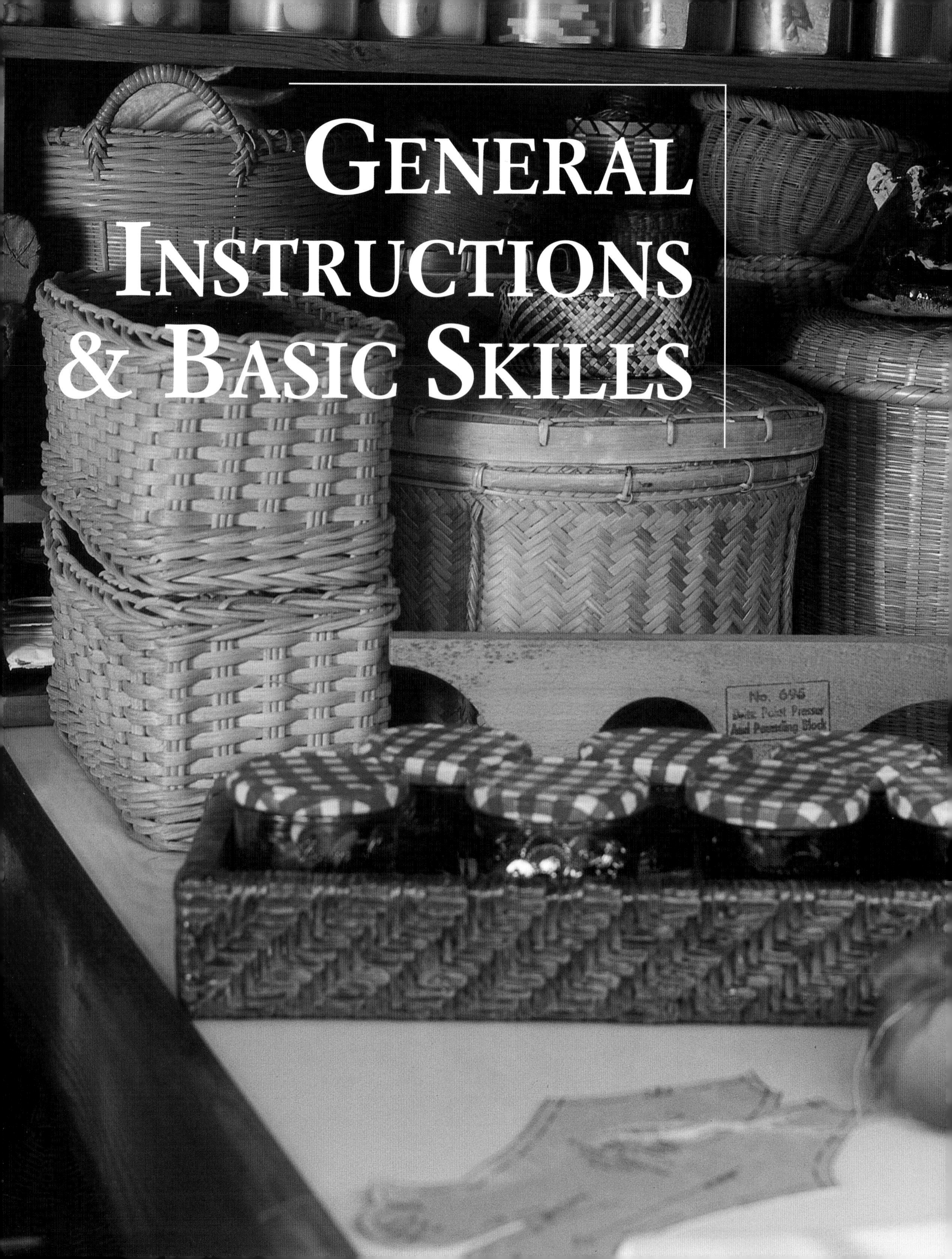

CHAPTER

2

BEFORE STARTING TO MAKE ANY DOLL, it is helpful to have a general understanding of the various stages of cutting, sewing, and stuffing required. While detailed instructions for making dolls and doll clothes are given in each chapter, there are general techniques that are common. This chapter should be read through before starting any of the projects, and is particularly helpful for beginner dollmakers and those unfamiliar with garment making. It can also be referred to as questions arise during construction.

Your talents will increase as you master the techniques shown and gain confidence in your abilities. Once you familiarize yourself with the specific techniques, feel free to be as inventive as you want. Experiment with new colors and materials, and relax and enjoy the creative process. With dollmaking, crafting the doll is as much fun as having the finished product.

THE PATTERN

Full-size pattern pieces for the doll and doll clothes are provided at the end of the book. Every pattern piece includes ¼" (6mm) seam allowances. Trace the patterns

Preparation

onto tracing paper, including all the markings, or photocopy them directly from the book. For longevity, use spray adhesive to affix the traced or copied patterns (except for the face) onto bristol board or thin cardboard and then cut them out. Trace the doll's face onto the face pattern piece.

THE FABRIC

It is not necessary to prewash most fabrics, however the chemical sizing applied to some fabrics can make it difficult for the fabric to accept dye. If you plan to dye the cloth, it is best to prewash it. On the other hand, sizing does provide a nice, crisp surface for applying paint and pencil. If you are unsure of how a fabric will behave and feel after washing, prewash a small scrap and observe whether it shrinks and how the hand of the cloth changes. If you do wash the fabric, apply spray starch as you press it to return some sizing back into the fabric.

Prior to laying out the pattern pieces, press fusible tricot to the wrong side of the uncut fabric for both the body and face of the doll. Treat the fabric and tricot as one during cutting and sewing.

LAYING OUT, MARKING & CUTTING

Lay out all the pattern pieces before cutting. Notice the grainline arrows on the pattern pieces and be sure to position those arrows along the lengthwise grain of all woven fabrics. Placing the pattern on-grain is necessary for the doll pieces go together properly and it helps the doll hang better. For knit fabrics, check which direction has the greatest degree of stretch and place the grainline in that direction.

Work on a hard surface. Pin the pattern pieces to the fabric, and cut around the indicated cutting lines. If the pattern pieces are too thick for pins, use pattern weights to hold the pattern pieces in position and trace around them with dressmaker's carbon and a tracing wheel, a pencil, or a disappearing fabric pen.

Use dressmaker's carbon paper or a disappearing fabric marker to transfer the pattern markings to the fabric. If the pattern is too thick for the markings to transfer through, use pins to pierce the fabric and then follow up by marking with a disappearing ink pen. Transfer the facial features (see chapter 4) onto the right side of the fabric with a ballpoint pen and carbon paper.

TIP: *It's faster and more accurate to trace around the pattern pieces with a pen or pencil.*

TIP: *To accurately sew the hands, particularly the reverse curve between the thumb and fingers, transfer the stitching line directly onto the fabric.*

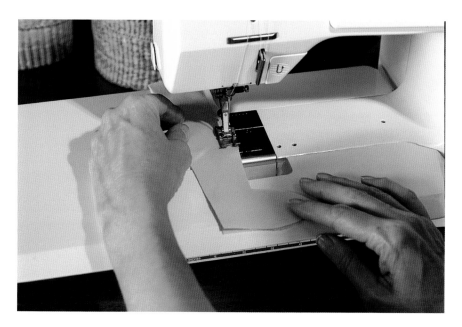

SEWING

Sew with ¼" (6mm) seam allowances and do not trim them unless the instructions indicate to do so. Since the seams are narrow, use a small-hole or straight-stitch throat plate to help keep the fabric from being pushed down into the machine. Switch to an all-purpose throat plate for zigzag stitching. Minimal pressing is required. A dowel is useful for pressing the small tight areas of the arms and legs. Finger-press seams that are too small or intricate to be pressed by an iron.

TIP: *When sewing doll dresses, overalls, or any garment with a separate bodice pattern piece, cut an extra set of bodice pieces and self-line the bodice for a clean finish. This is particularly a good idea when sewing with thin cotton or fine linen.*

Fabulous-looking trim is quick and easy to make. Here are a variety of trim ideas that can be used to enhance and vary the style of any basic pattern.

Trim Ideas

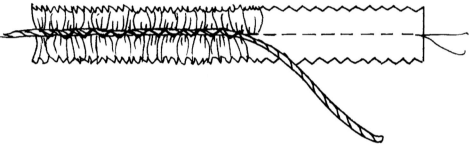

1. Cut a ⅞" (2.2cm)-wide strip of polyester or silk taffeta, and then trim all of the edges with pinking scissors. Run a gathering stitch through the center of the strip. Pull the gathering stitch to rouch the fabric, and then zigzag cording directly over the gathering. This trim is particularly nice for hats, bags, and garments.

2. Run a loose zigzag stitch down the center of narrow ribbon. Pull the threads to rouch the ribbon; secure the short ends. Straight stitch directly over the gathering stitches to secure them in place.

3. Run a gathering stitch down the center of narrow ribbon. Pull the threads to gather the ribbon and secure the ends. With a decorative or embroidery stitch, sew directly over the gathering.

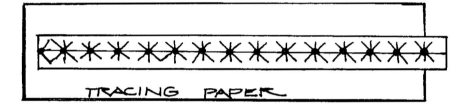

4. Sew machine embroidery stitches down the center of narrow ribbon or bias tape. Place tissue paper under the trim to create a smooth, wide surface for sewing. Tear away the tissue paper after sewing.

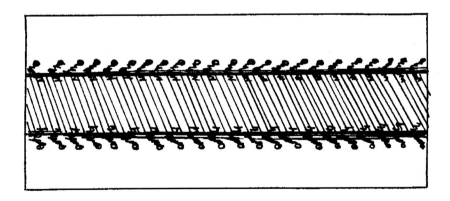

5. Stitch wide ribbon to the lower edge or within the body of a garment with a hemstitch and decorative thread, or any embroidery stitch.

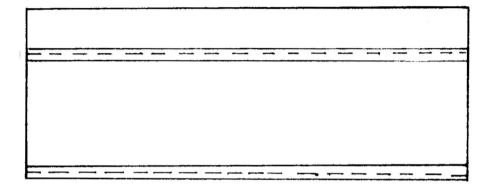

6. For a sheer effect, attach organza ribbon to a garment edge and press the seam allowances toward the garment.

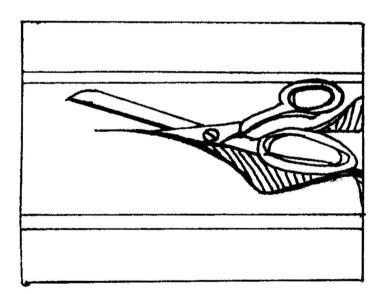

7. For an inlaid effect, stitch the ribbon in place along both long edges. Cut through the fabric in the middle of the ribbon.

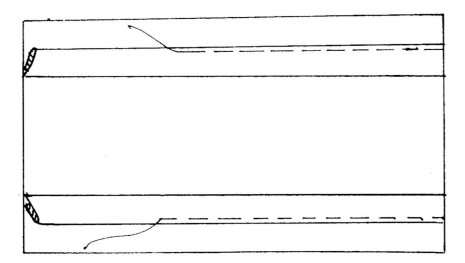

Fold each side of the fabric over and over again toward the edge of the ribbon. Stitch the folded fabric in place.

8. For an elegant finish, use a pearl presser foot and monofilament thread to attach pearls or crystal beads onto ready-made trim, or hand-sew them in place. Try tracing a design onto the fabric and applying the beads over the tracing.

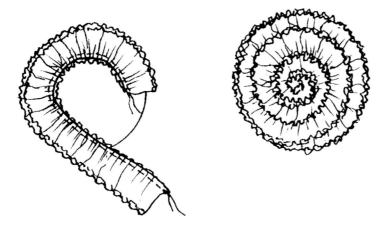

9. For a gathered ribbon rosette, run gathering stitches along one long end of a length of ribbon. Pull the stitches so the ribbon folds into itself, forming a circle. Continue pulling the stitches and folding the ribbon to form a rosette. With a hand needle, stitch the ribbon onto a circle of non-woven pellon, folding and stitching to form the flower.

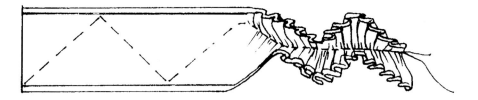

10. Apply gathering stitches in a zigzag pattern across the width of a length of ribbon. Pull the threads to form a zigzag ruffle. Apply the ruffle to the garment directly over the gathering stitches.

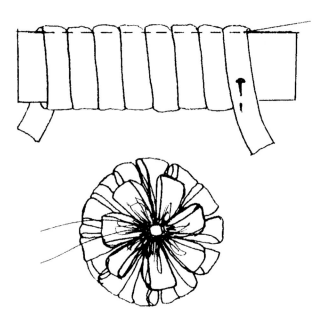

11. For a pleated ribbon rosette, cut two widths of cardboard, 1" (2.5cm) and ½" (1.3cm). Wrap a length of ribbon around each piece of cardboard and hand-sew gathering stitches across the top of each. Slide out the cardboard and pull the stitches to form two separate rosettes. Secure the gathering stitches and hand-sew the smaller rosette over the larger in the center. With the same thread, attach the rosette to the garment.

BACKSTITCH: Secure threads at end of stitching by straight-stitching in reverse.

Sewing Terms

BIAS: Diagonal intersection, 45 degrees from the lengthwise and crosswise grain.

BLINDSTITCH: For hemming, use a blindstitch concealed between two layers of fabric. Turn fabric edge down about ¼" (6mm). Make a small diagonal stitch by first picking up one thread of garment, then one thread of hem; repeat. To blindstitch by machine, turn up hem; fold garment back about ¼"-⅜" (6-10mm) beyond hem edge. Position fabric on machine so needle catches only one thread of folded edge.

CLEAN FINISH: Simple seam finishes that add durability to an item and give it a neater inside appearance. Doll seams should not be clean finished, as it would add bulk and show through; however, the doll clothes can be clean finished. There are several suitable clean finishes described below. For each, stitch the seam and press it open.

Turn and Stitch: Turn each seam edge under and edgestitch.

Pink and Stitch: Stitch along each seam allowance, and then pink the edges with pinking shears.

Zigzag: Zigzag over the raw edge of each seam allowance.

Serged: If you have serger, simply finish the raw edges with a basic serger stitch.

EASESTITCH: Stitch along the seamline, using long machine stitches, approximately six to eight stitches per inch (2.5cm). Leave 6" (15cm) thread ends at each end of the stitching. Do not backstitch at either end. Pull the thread ends to adjust the fit.

EDGESTITCH: Stitch close to a finished edge or seam with a regular stitch.

FINGER PRESSING: Instead of using an iron, run finger along seamline and fold line to press.

GATHER: Using long machine stitches, stitch along the seamline and again ⅛" (3mm) away in the seam allowance. Leave 6" (15cm) thread ends at each end of the stitching. Pull the thread ends from one end to gather; adjust the gathers to fit.

GRAIN: Direction in which the fabric threads run.

Lengthwise grain: Fabric threads running parallel to the selvage.

Crosswise grain: Fabric threads running perpendicular to the lengthwise grain and selvage.

INTERFACING: A fabric used to add body and opacity to decorative fabric.

NARROW HEM: Useful for hemming sheer fabrics and small doll clothes. Turn in ¼" (6mm); press, easing fullness if necessary. Open out hem. Turn in again so raw edge is along pressed crease; press. Turn in along first crease; stitch.

REINFORCE: Small machine stitches stitched along the seamline for extra security.

SELVAGE: The tightly-woven, finished border along both lengthwise sides of fabric, usually about ¼" (6mm) to ½" (1.3cm) wide.

SLIPSTITCH: A hand stitch commonly used for closing an opening that was used for turning. Slide your needle through one folded edge for approximately ¼" (6mm), then through the opposite folded edge, drawing the thread so that the two edges meet. To hem, slide your needle through the inner folded edge of the hem approximately ¼" (6mm), then pick up a thread or two from the fabric behind the hem.

STAYSTITCH: A machine stitch done prior to joining two pieces to prevent stretching along a cut edge. Using small machine stitches, stitch just inside the seamline.

TOPSTITCH: A decorative or functional stitch. Using desired machine stitch length, stitch ¼" (6mm) from the edge or seam, using your presser foot as a guide if possible. (Most sewing machines measure ¼" (6mm) from the needle position to the side edge of the presser foot, so it makes a handy guide.)

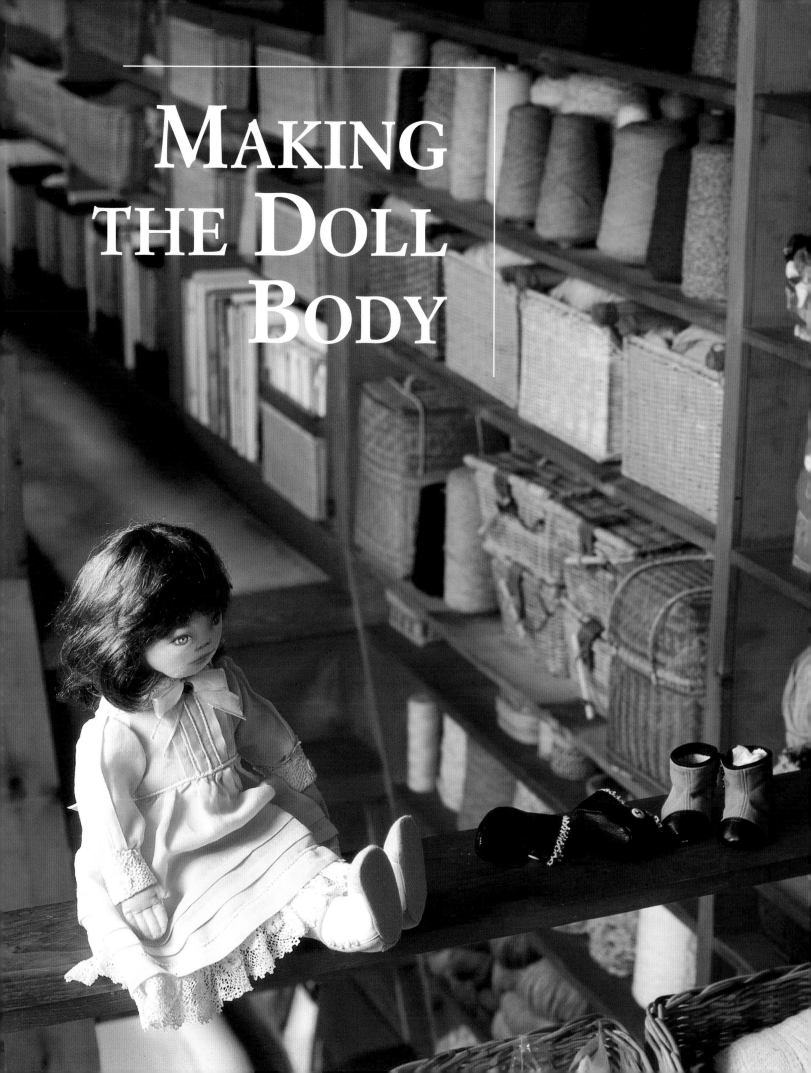

MAKING THE DOLL BODY

CHAPTER
3

HERE BEGINS AN EXCITING journey into dollmaking! Whether you are a novice or an experienced dollmaker, you will find this beautifully photographed step-by-step guide informative and enlightening. The easy-to-follow illustrations and text demonstrate simple sewing techniques and share the knowledge gained from years of dollmaking experience. Learn about the importance of pivoting and clipping, how multiple pins help ease fabric, and the best way to position fabric in the sewing machine to facilitate sewing curves. Best of all, learn how to turn flat fabric into a dimensional doll body. Even before the doll is stuffed, you will see it come to life as each step gives shape and form to the fabric!

YOU WILL NEED:

Fabric:

Doll body: ⅝ yd (.6m) of 45" (115cm) woven fabric

Doll face: 5" x 6" (12.5cm x 15cm) knit fabric remnant

Fusible tricot: ¼ yd (.7m) to line body and face

Notions:

10 oz. (300 grams) polyester fiberfill

5" x 3" (12.5cm x 7.5cm) cardboard remnant

paper-backed fusible web

Tools:

Dressmaker's carbon paper, ballpoint pen, straight pins, disappearing ink pen, small scissors, seam roll, iron, dowel or blunt knitting needle or stuffing tool

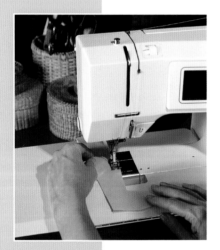

Begin with the front legs. With the right sides of the fabric together, stitch two FRONT LEG pieces together, as shown. Pivot at the ankle, indicated by the small •. Stop stitching at the large •, near the toe. Reinforce the stitching at the ankle pivot point to strengthen the seam at this important body curve. Repeat with the remaining front leg pieces.

STEP 1

TIP: *Reinforce stitches at every pivot point by shortening the stitch length for about ½" (1.3cm) each side of the pivot point or by backstitching two times on either side of the pivot point.*

Clip diagonally at the ankle, indicated by the small •. In order for the doll's leg to turn properly, it is very important to clip right up to, but not through the stitching. Press the seam open; use a seam roll to press the curved, foot section of the seam. Repeat with the remaining front leg pieces.

STEP 2

TIP: *To clip into seam allowances, use small scissors and do not open them all the way. Only cut with the tips of the scissors to prevent accidentally clipping through the stitching.*

TIP: *Very few steps require using an iron. Unless otherwise indicated, finger pressing is adequate.*

With the right sides of the fabric together, pin one front leg to the lower edge of the doll BODY FRONT piece, with the side seams aligned and the inner leg • matching the center front •. Stitch from the side seam to the inner leg • so that the seam allowance is not caught in the stitching; backstitch. Pin the remaining leg to the body front so that the side seams and small inner •'s align. Stitch from the side seam to the inner leg •, as with the first leg; backstitch.

STEP 3

TIP: *There is a break in the stitching at the center front point, however from the front the seam appears unbroken.*

Prepare the BACK LEGS by reinforcing the inner leg area. To reinforce, stitch along the inseam, shortening the stitch length as the needle nears the pivot point, as shown. Do not clip the inner leg seam allowance at this time. Stitch the darts in both legs to create the shape of the calves.

STEP 4

With the right sides of the fabric together, stitch the doll BODY BACK pieces together below the small •. Finger-press the seam open. Pin the back legs to the lower edge of the body back with the right sides of the fabric together and the center of the legs aligned with the center of the body; stitch. Finger-press the seam toward the legs.

STEP

5

Stitch the shoulder darts in both ARM pieces. Finger-press the darts open.

STEP

6

TIP: *As you approach the end of the dart, take the last few stitches along the fold of the fabric to ease the stitching right off the edge of the fabric.*

With the right sides of the fabric together, pin the arm sections to the front and back of the doll body, matching the small •'s, as shown; stitch.

STEP 7

TIP: *The curve between the thumb and the fingers is a reverse curve. If you haven't already done so, it is helpful and more accurate to mark this stitching line with a disappearing ink pen before sewing.*

Place the front and back doll body pieces together with the right sides of the fabric together. Pin the side seams, including the under arm edges and hands. The horizontal seams on the front and back body pieces do not match up because of the contour of the body. Use a generous supply of pins for added accuracy. Starting at the ankle, stitch each side in one continuous seam.

STEP 8

As the needle approaches the small • at the thumb point, shorten the stitch length and gently pivot, taking care to follow the marked seamline. Continue sewing the seam around the fingers to the outer wrist. Run the stitching along the fold at the wrist for several stitches.

STEP 9

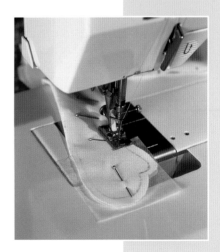

TIP: *To help stitch small curved areas like the thumb and fingers, slide a piece of tissue paper under the fabric and stitch right through the fabric and tissue paper. After stitching, tear the tissue paper away.*

To ensure well-shaped hands, clip to the inner small • near the thumb and trim the seam allowance to ⅛" (3mm) from wrist to wrist, going around the thumb and the fingers.

STEP

10

With the right sides of the fabric together, stitch the inner leg seam. Curve the pivot point slightly into a tight U-shape by taking one or two horizontal stitches across the pivot point. Slash up to, but not through stitching.

STEP

11

Make a small snip at the center back of each leg. Make a second small snip ⅛" (3mm) away from first. Do not make the snip more than ⅛" (3mm) away or it will weaken the seam. Pin one SOLE piece to the lower edge of one leg, with the right sides of the fabric together and the symbols matching. Use enough pins to ease the sole into the foot. Hold the doll body so that the foot and sole pieces rest slightly upright on the machine bed and stitch the seam from the top. Trim the entire seam allowance to ⅛" (3mm). Repeat with the remaining sole piece. Smooth the sole seams with your fingers to make room for the cardboard inserts.

STEP
12

Turn the doll body right side out. Use a dowel or blunt knitting needle to carefully poke out the thumb and fingers. Using the GUIDE FOR CARDBOARD, cut two pieces of white cardboard and two pieces of paper-backed fusible web to add to the base of each foot for support.

STEP
13

TIP: *If the cardboard is lightweight, cut four pieces and insert a second piece in each foot after the first piece is in place, or use foam core instead of cardboard for additional support.*

With a moderately hot iron, fuse one piece of web to each piece of cardboard or foam core. Let the fusible web cool, and then remove the backing. Insert the cardboard inserts into each foot with the web side down so it rests against the fabric. Smooth the seams so that the seam allowances point toward the body and do not rest on the soles of the feet. Use pins to hold the seam even with the edges of the cardboard to ensure smooth, even feet.

STEP
14

With a slightly hotter iron, apply heat to the soles of the feet to fuse the cardboard in place. This creates a firm, smooth sole and makes it easier to stuff the doll legs.

STEP
15

TIP: *Make sure the pins are not protruding out onto the fabric, or else the iron could leave pin imprints on the fabric.*

Go over the markings for the fingers. It is best to mark with pins and then fill in the stitching lines with a disappearing ink pen. The fingers are stuffed at this point in order to finish sewing the doll body.

STEP
16

TIP: *Work with a minimal amount of fiberfill; you can always add more. The size of a quarter is about right for the fingers.*

Insert fiberfill into the fingers. Use a pin to pull the fiberfill right up to the seamline and to help smooth the curved edge. Sew the center finger line first, smoothing the fiberfill in both directions. Backstitch at both ends of the stitching. Stitch the remaining two finger markings. Do not overstuff the fingers, they are not meant to be as firm as the arms, legs, and body.

STEP
17

TIP: *For extra-secure finger stitching, begin sewing at the outer edge of the hand and stitch along the marked line. At the end of the marking, pivot the doll around and stitch directly over the previous stitches back to the fingertips.*

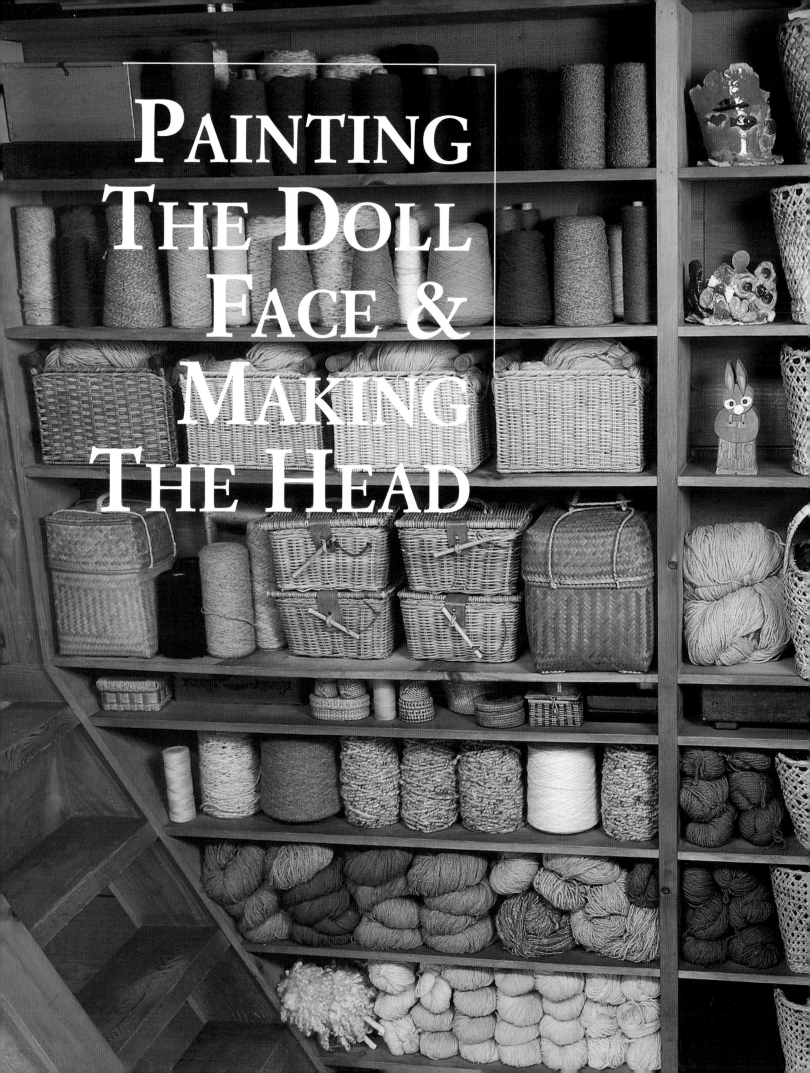

Painting The Doll Face & Making The Head

CHAPTER

4

ONE OF THE MOST EXCITING aspects of making your own doll is painting her or his face, for it is here that you create the doll's unique personality! The following instructions and photographs clearly show the way to bestow depth, interest, and character to a flat piece of fabric using simple coloring tools, such as colored pencils, drugstore blush and eye shadow, and just a bit of black and white acrylic paint. Follow the easy, step-by-step instructions as they transform blank fabric to a full-color, charmingly sweet face. Just compare the first and last photographs and you'll be amazed at the difference!

As it's a good idea to practice any new skill, you should first paint faces on paper and scrap fabric, until you feel confident enough in your skills to paint the "real" doll face. It helps to look at photographs of real people to get a sense of facial features and a feel for the nuances of natural shading. The face requires such a small piece of fabric that if you make a mistake you can simply start over. In fact, it's a good idea to make several fabric faces so you can experiment with different shades of colored pencils until you find the look you desire. Consider substituting light blue, green, or amber for the yellow pencil and shades of peach in place of the coral pencils.

Use the full-color photograph of the painted doll's face as a reference as you follow the detailed instructions to paint your own. Work on a firm surface for stability and support, with plenty of light to ensure that the coloring is neither too strong, nor too pale.

YOU WILL NEED:

Materials:
Dressmaker's carbon paper, ballpoint pen, pencil sharpener, bristol board or heavy cardboard, cotton swabs, hair spray or clear acrylic spray, temporary spray adhesive, straight pins

Painting Supplies:
#2 lead pencil

PrismaColor® Colored Pencils—Canary Yellow #916, Sienna Brown #945, Burnt Henna #1034, Pale Coral #926, Pink Rose #1018, Peach #939

Two colors of blush, beige eye shadow, and a makeup brush

Black and white acrylic paint

#2, #4, #7 paintbrushes

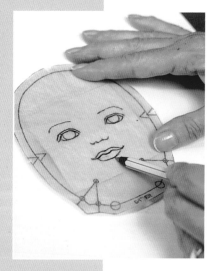

Trace the facial features onto the FACE pattern piece. Use dressmaker's carbon paper and a fine ballpoint pen to transfer the facial features from the pattern piece to the face fabric. Practice on a piece of scrap fabric first to get a feel for how hard you have to push on the pen to make markings that are dark enough to see, but not so dark that they will show through the paint. Use temporary spray adhesive to secure the fabric for the face onto a piece of bristol board or heavy cardboard to make it easier to paint. Tape the board to a firm work surface to prevent it from slipping. Position a small square of dressmaker's carbon paper between the pattern and the fabric.

STEP

1

TIP: *When transferring markings, particularly the facial features, work on a firm surface such as a pad of paper or a board.*

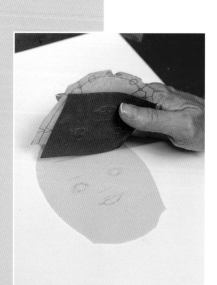

Transfer the markings for the eyes, nose, and mouth. Do not transfer the darts, notches, or outline of the face at this time. Peel back a corner of the carbon paper to make sure the transferred markings are clearly visible. Take care not to disturb the position of the pattern on the fabric. Remove the pattern piece and the carbon paper, but keep the face fabric adhered to the background board for stability.

STEP

2

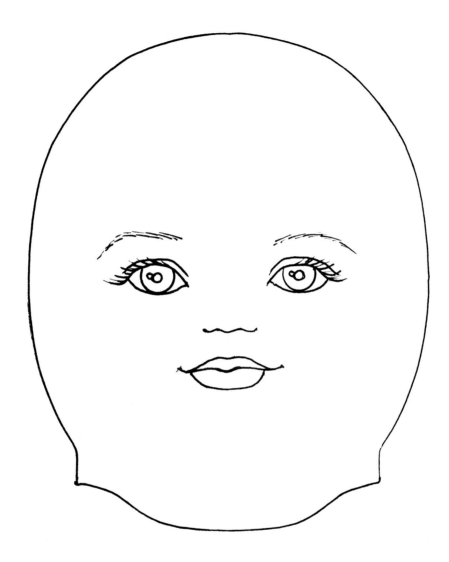

Using short strokes and the SIENNA BROWN #945 pencil, lightly retrace all the carbon-marked lines, except the eye pupil. Do not take long strokes, as they tend to drag the fabric. Work short, feathery strokes for the eyebrow to create the resemblance of a real eyebrow.

STEP

3

TIP: *Use a light touch—you can always add more.*

Paint the entire inside of each eye with white acrylic paint and a fine #4 paintbrush. Paint up to, but not over the marked lines of the eye pupils. Apply enough paint so that the eyes look totally opaque. Let the paint dry before proceeding to the next step.

STEP

4

TIP: *It is very important to let the paint dry completely before adding any more makeup or paint.*

Using a #7 paintbrush, apply pale beige eye shadow along the inner and outside curves of each eye. For the inner corners, work the shadow onto the fabric from the eyebrow down along the nose. Avoid excess color over the center of the eye; however, a light stroke across the top lid line does add depth. At the outside corners, feather the eye shadow out and up to the eyebrow, intensifying the color slightly. With a clean cotton swab, add blush directly on top of the eye shadow to create natural-looking eyes.

STEP 5

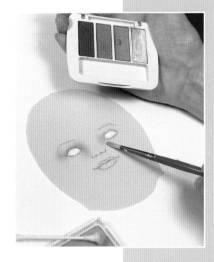

TIP: *With a feathery application, form a crescent shape along the inner corner of the eye.*

TIP: *To make the eye appear more lifelike, use a clean cotton swab to blend and smooth the eye shadow. A clean swab can also be used to wipe off excess makeup without smearing or distorting. Blending the makeup is the only way to create a natural, even-looking face, especially when working with two shades of color or different types of makeup.*

With a minimal amount of blush on a #7 paintbrush, use a light touch to sweep across the bottom of the nose. The natural shape of the brush makes it easy to create a soft line (unlike the hard line made with a pencil). Retrace the marked lines of the nose with the BURNT HENNA #1034 pencil, intensifying the features. Add one small dot in each nostril and blend. Use a clean cotton swab to apply a little more blush over the nose to soften and blend the colors.

STEP 6

Using a makeup brush, apply a brighter shade of blush to the cheeks with a dabbing motion. Add enough color to give the face a ruddy, natural glow, then rub and blend the blush into the fabric with a cotton swab. Continue blending over and around the cheekbones to form a round apple shape where the color is most intense. Then, with the makeup brush, blend the blush out toward the edge of the fabric, lightening the color as it gets closer to the fabric edge. Extend the blush through the seam allowances to avoid a hard line of makeup.

STEP 7

Using the makeup brush, lightly apply the same bright blush in a sweeping, U-shape motion across the top of the forehead, working from the outside of one eyebrow to the outside of the opposite eyebrow. Add color to the entire forehead, extending out as far as the seam allowances. Blend with a cotton swab from temple to temple. Using the same sweeping motion, apply blush 1" (2.5cm) down from the lips in a slightly flatter U-shape curve around the chin. Blend with a cotton swab.

STEP

8

With soft, feathery strokes, color in the upper and lower lips with the PINK ROSE #1018 or PEACH #939 pencil. Color directly over the previously marked lip lines. With the darker, BURNT HENNA #1034 pencil, draw feathery strokes in three areas of the lips to create depth. Begin with short, feathery strokes along the lower edge of the lower lip, making it darkest in the center of the lip. With the same pencil, retrace the line where the two lips meet working straight across with a feathery, brushlike application. Intensify the color on either side of the dip in the center of the mouth. Add diagonal shadow strokes from the top of the upper lip to the bottom of the upper lip. To duplicate the natural shape of the mouth, keep the strokes slightly off center so they end near the dip in the center of the mouth.

STEP

9

Because the white paint covers the previous markings, use the pattern as a guide and redraw the pupils of each eye with the BURNT HENNA #1034 pencil. (For clarity, use a regular #2 pencil to redraw the pupils of each eye. Sometimes it is possible to get a sharper point on a regular pencil than on a colored pencil.) Intensify the color along the sides of each pupil with the Burnt Henna pencil. With the CANARY YELLOW #916 pencil, color in the pupil of each eye, leaving the Burnt Henna outline visible.

STEP 10

TIP: *For the most natural-looking eye, draw a curved line along both sides of each pupil. Do not draw a full circle around the entire pupil.*

TIP: *To change the color of the eyes, substitute the yellow pencil with a light blue or green colored pencil.*

Use the SIENNA BROWN #945 pencil to retrace the outlines of the eyes, including the pupils. Add the most intense color near the top, lightening it slightly and arching it toward the sides in a half-moon shape. In the lower eye area, draw several, small radiating lines extending from the iris downward. Trace over the eyelid crease line with same pencil. To create upper and lower eyelashes, draw flicking little lines radiating outward from the eyes. Use the same flicking motion on eyebrow markings to thicken the existing eyebrows.

STEP 11

TIP: *For more dramatic eyelashes, use black paint or a fine-tip, black permanent marker instead of a colored pencil.*

With a minimal
amount of black
acrylic paint and a #2
paintbrush, dab one
dot in the center of
each eye. The dot does not need to
be perfectly round since additional
white paint is added later.

STEP
12

TIP: *Make several test dots on scrap*
fabric to determine how much paint
you need on the brush—a very small
amount is usually sufficient.

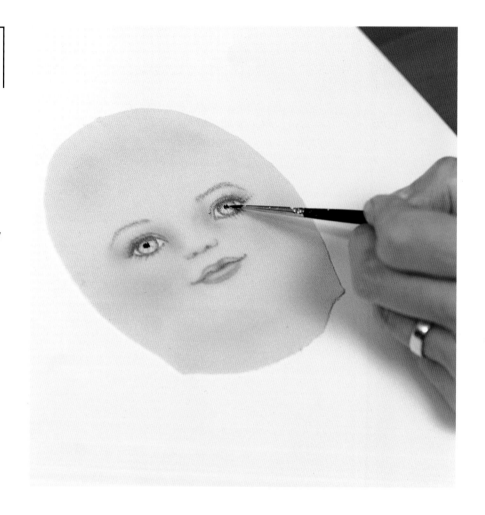

With a #2 paintbrush and a very small amount of white paint,
dab two dots of white paint in each eye. Make sure the white dots
fall on either side and slightly over the edges of the black dot. Add
an additional white dot slightly to the right or left of the center of
the nose, over and between the two dark pencil dots. Add two
more white dots on the lower lip. Position the dots to the right and left of
the center, then smudge the paint slightly between the dots.

STEP
13

Examine the completed face; add or remove makeup until you are satisfied. Once the face is finished and all the paint is dry, spray the face lightly with hair spray or clear acrylic spray to prevent the makeup and paint from rubbing off and to protect the face from abrasion.

STEP
14

TIP: *When using hair spray, apply two or three coats, letting each coat dry completely before adding the next one. Acrylic spray requires only one coat.*

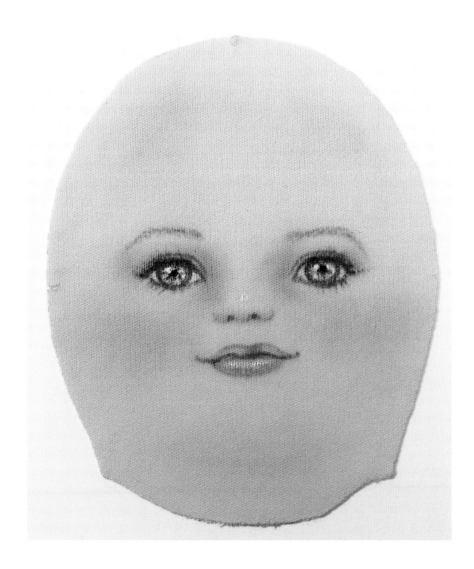

Referring to the face pattern piece, transfer the neck dart markings onto the wrong side of the face fabric. Use a disappearing ink pen to connect the markings. Sew the darts, then carefully slash them and press them open.

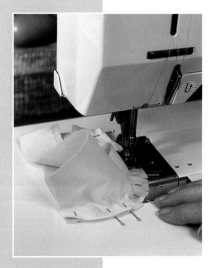

With right sides together, pin the two HEAD SIDE pieces to the HEAD CENTER piece, matching the notches. Stitch the seams and clip the curves. Press the seams flat and then toward the head center.

TIP: *Use a generous number of pins around the curves. Before you stitch the seam, clip ⅛" (3mm) into the seam allowance between the pins to help the fabric lay flat.*

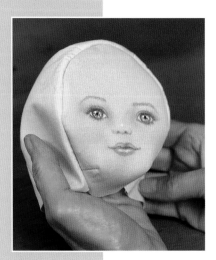

Pin the face to the head with right sides together and matching the symbols. Use a generous amount of pins to help ease the pieces together. Stitch between the two large •'s, leaving the neck edge open. Turn the head right side out and smooth the seam with your fingers.

Pin the NECK to the lower edge of the head with right sides together and symbols aligned; stitch.

With right sides together, pin the lower neck edge to the body and stitch.

Turn the doll head and neck wrong side out (do not turn the entire body wrong side out—it's not necessary). Pin the center back seam from the marking below the neck, through the neck and up to the top of the head, shaping it like a dart until it meets the head center piece. Place pins in both neck seam allowances so they both face upward. The center back of the doll body remains open so you can stuff the doll. Stitch the pinned seam, then backstitch to secure the stitching for stuffing.

STUFFING & FINISHING

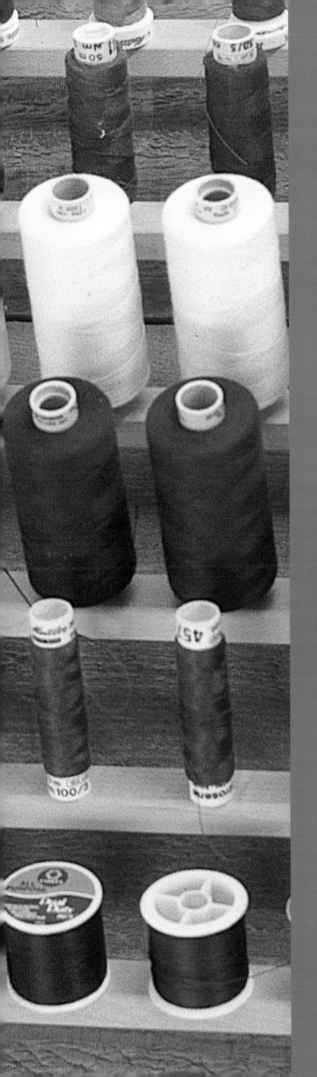

CHAPTER

5

PROPER STUFFING TECHNIQUE IS CRUCIAL to a good-looking, long-lasting doll. So, instead of one quick step merely indicating that you stuff the doll, this chapter devotes several steps to the process, each clearly demonstrating how to professionally stuff each body part. Novice and even experienced dollmakers tend to understuff and not smooth the stuffing enough for a seamless body. Take the time to follow each step—the results are well worth it!

As a general rule, add a small amount of stuffing at a time so that beginnings and endings are not visible. As you stuff, check for lumps on the outer surface and use your hands to shape and mold the various sections. Smooth creases by adding more stuffing and pushing it firmly into each crease. Stuffing does tend to settle down or contract over time, so if in doubt, use more rather than less.

After the doll is stuffed, only the finishing touches remain. First, give your doll hair. Choose from the many beautiful doll wigs available, or use yarn to create the hairstyle of your choice. Add ears to a boy doll or a doll with a short hairstyle, and sew the doll closed. Once your doll is finished, name him or her, sign your name, and then enjoy your creation!

YOU WILL NEED:

Tools:
Two 6" (15cm) dowels, ¼" (6mm) diameter
A ruler, wide dowel, blunt pencil,
or stuffing tool
Sewing needle
Buttonhole twist
Scissors
Permanent ink pen
Straight pins

Materials:
Approximately 8.8 oz. (241 grams) polyester
fiberfill
One 12" (30.5cm) purchased doll wig to fit 18"
(46cm) doll or one skein of mohair-like yarn

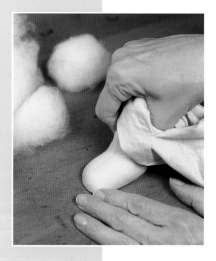

Separate the fiberfill by pulling the fibers into tennis-size balls. Begin by stuffing the feet. Use your thumb to push the fiberfill into each toe. Use your other hand to shape, mold, and pull the fabric as you push the fiberfill in place. Once the toes are packed, move to the heels and then the ankles. Pack the fiberfill firmly and continue adding it to make firm, smooth feet. If there are creases around the ankles, push additional fiberfill into the creases to smooth them out.

STEP

1

TIP: *It is crucial to stuff the ankles very firmly to prevent them from giving way when the doll stands.*

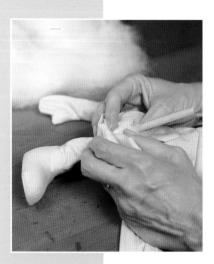

If you wish to have a doll that stands or sits with firm, out-stretched legs, insert a 6" (15cm) dowel in the center of each leg. (If you prefer a more floppy doll, simply leave the dowels out.) If finding the center proves difficult, favor the inside of the leg over the outside of the leg. Push the dowel down into the stuffed foot until it is about ¾" (2cm) from the bottom. Hold the dowel in place and insert fiberfill all around it. Because the legs are larger than the feet, work with slightly larger pieces of fiberfill (make each piece about the size of a softball). Use the flat edge of a ruler, a wide dowel, or a blunt pencil to push and pack the fiberfill. Shape and mold the leg with your hands. Fill each leg to just below the front (not the back) leg-to-body seam.

STEP

2

TIP: *Push and pack fiberfill firmly into the back leg darts to contour and shape the back calf muscles.*

Stuff the arms much like the legs, but eliminate the dowels. Use the edge of a ruler or a dowel to pack the stuffing firmly and smoothly. Work the fiberfill into the hands and down to the fingers. Do not add more fiberfill to the fingers—they should not be stuffed as firmly as the rest of the hand. Also, do not pack fiberfill into the thumb; keep it flexible, more like the fingers. Continue stuffing and shaping the arms up to the body seam.

STEP 3

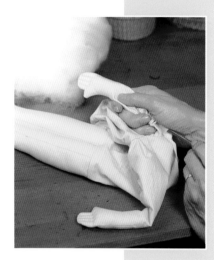

To stuff the head, start with a piece of fiberfill the size of a small plate, and about 1" (2.5cm) thick. Use your hands to round and smooth the fiberfill into the shape of a small grapefruit half. Insert the shaped fiberfill directly behind the face to ensure a smooth surface. Fill the rest of the face area, packing firmly. Move the seam allowances away from the face, toward the back of the head. Continue filling the head with large, baseball-size pieces of fiberfill. Stuff from behind, pushing fiberfill up to the smooth face area.

STEP 4

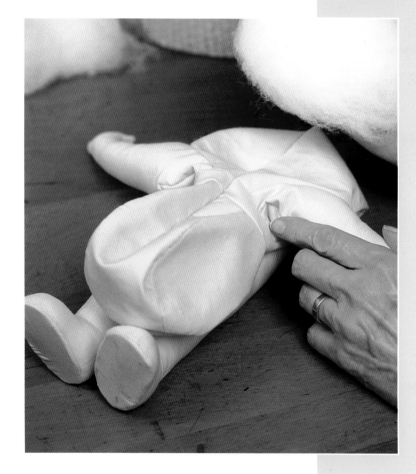

TIP: *To shape and fill out the top of the head, hold the doll's head like a baseball and push the fiberfill into your hand. Think of the top of the head as a ball and mold the fiberfill with your palm to create a slightly domed forehead.*

TIP: *It is very important to pack the fiberfill firmly throughout the doll. Take special care with the head and neck. Like the ankles, the head and neck need to be very firmly stuffed to support the weight of the doll. If in doubt, add more fiberfill.*

After the head is stuffed, shape the chin by adding more fiber-fill between the darts. Use your thumb or the stuffing tool to push the chin out and away from the neck. The area of the chin below the apex of the darts should be flat to create a strong-looking, slightly domed chin.

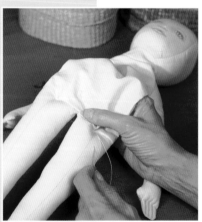

If you want the doll to sit, joint the legs with hand tacks. Use the buttonhole twist or four strands of regular sewing thread. Pinch the leg at the front leg-to-body seam, so that the front touches the back. Knot the thread and insert it from the back. Pull the thread to the front and take a small horizontal stitch about ⅛" (3mm) wide. Go over the first stitch several times, pulling each stitch tightly. Cut the thread without knotting it. The back knot is buried in the stitches. Repeat on the remaining leg.

If you wish to joint the arms (it is not necessary), pinch the arm at the marking so that the underarm seam touches the outside of the arm. Insert the knotted thread from the underarm and pull the thread through to the outside of the arm. Make several stitches directly over the first stitch. Pull the stitches very tightly and cut the thread. Repeat for the remaining arm.

STEP
7

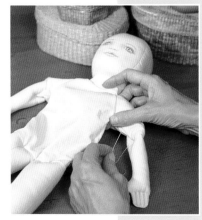

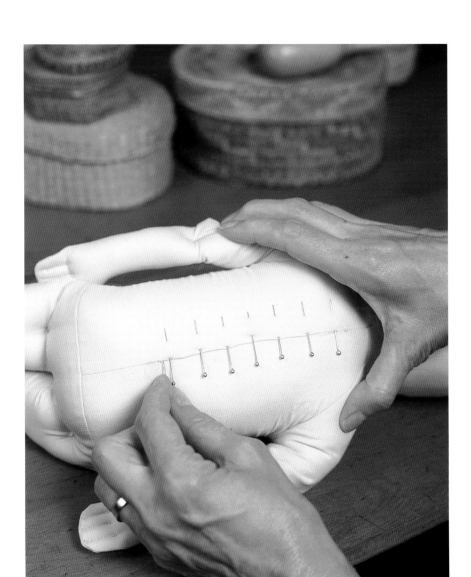

Stuff the rest of the doll. Avoid overstuffing the joints, or the doll will not be as flexible as you would probably like. Pack the stuffing firmly to fill out the buttocks and to give the shoulders a slightly domed shape. Once the doll is completely stuffed, abut the center back seams and pin them closed. Blindstitch the doll closed by hand.

STEP
8

TIP: *Once the whole doll is made, you may find you want to go back and apply more color to the cheeks and forehead. Feel free!*

TIP: *If you feel there is too much contrast between the face and body fabrics, extend the blush beyond the face onto the back of the head and the neck.*

Position the doll wig on the doll head so that it covers the seam between the head and the face. Hold the wig in place with pins. Hand-sew the elastic band of the wig to the entire circumference of the doll's head, stretching the elastic band to cover the seam.

STEP
9

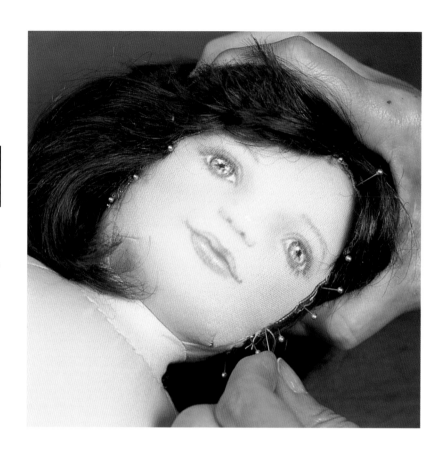

To make hair from yarn, begin by winding the whole skein of yarn around the back of a chair. Cut the ends to make long, flat strands. Working with five to six strands at a time, cut the yarn into 4½" (11.5cm) chunks. Starting at the base of the head, around the hairline, sew a chunk of yarn onto the head. Use small back-stitches in the middle of each chunk and give the thread a good tug to secure it. After stitching, pull the ends of the yarn up and then fold them downward to make room for subsequent chunks of yarn. Continue in this manner sewing chunks of yarn in rows or circles 1" (2.5cm) to 1½" (3.8cm) apart all around the head. Cover the entire surface, working from the neck to the crown. The circles get smaller as you reach the top of the head. No fabric should be visible through the yarn.

STEP
10

TIP: *Use carpet thread or four strands of regular thread to attach the yarn to the head. Textured yarn covers the best.*

For a boy or shorthaired doll, cut four EAR pieces from the body fabric. With the right sides of the fabric together, stitch two sections together, leaving the edge with the symbols open. Trim the seam allowance. Repeat with the remaining two sections. Turn the ears right side out and press. Baste the raw edges together. Topstitch around the finished edge of each ear, ⅛" (3mm) from the edge. Pin each ear against the face/head seam so the unfinished edge of each ear is ¼" (6mm) over the seam and the right side of the ear is down. Note that the curve of the ear points toward the face. Hand-sew the ear in place directly over the face/head seam. Clip and trim the seam allowance. Fold each ear toward the back of the head so that the topstitching is visible. Pinch the ear slightly to give it a dimple in the middle and tack the outside edge of the ear to the doll's head.

STEP 11

TIP: *The ears should be positioned between the eyes and the mouth. Adjust the ears before sewing until you are pleased with the appearance.*

TIP: *Dust the ear with a little blush so it matches the face.*

Lightly brush all the hair downward and then give the doll a haircut. Leave the yarn on the top of the head a little longer than the rest—just trim the ends to neaten. Cut the hair around the ears and the back of the head as needed to shape and style.

STEP 12

Name your doll and sign your name with a permanent ink marker!

STEP 13

MAKING DOLL CLOTHES & ACCESSORIES

CHAPTER

6

The fun continues! Now you get to dress your doll…dress her the way you would like to dress, the way you wouldn't dare to dress, or in a salute to the past! This chapter includes patterns and instructions to make beautiful period ensembles, as well as more modern attire. There are six complete outfits, ranging from charming undergarments to an outerwear cape and hat—a total of seventeen pieces in all that can be mixed and matched as desired. After you've finished sewing this complete wardrobe, check the *Vogue Pattern Book* for more Linda Carr patterns for doll clothes and accessories to fit this adorable eighteen-inch doll.

If desired, you can use these patterns as a jumping-off point to design your own, one-of-a-kind doll clothes. Look through books, magazines, and all around you for inspiration. Shop tag sales and antique shops for beautiful fabrics, buttons, and trims. Keep a box of odds and ends, small notions, trinkets, charms—any precious little item that can be used to create novelty decorations and accessories.

Most of the notions that are required to make these doll clothes are available through traditional retail outlets, as well as from the suppliers listed on the resources page. Even so, you may find that it is easier and more fun to make some of the trims yourself! Refer to chapter two for trim suggestions, as well as for trim-making tips.

FESTIVE FINERY

This dainty dress-up outfit, featuring a dress, bloomers, boots, and tights, is a must-have for any doll's wardrobe.

YOU WILL NEED:

FABRIC:

Dress & Bloomers:
1 yd. (.95m) of 45" (115cm) fabric—woolens, organdy, fine cotton, silk, velveteen, linen

Tights:
⅜ yd. (.4m) of 45" (115cm) fabric—two-way stretch knit

Boots:
¼ yd. (.25m) or a 7" x 12" (18cm x 30.5cm) scrap of linen, broadcloth, felt, ultrasuede, leather

4" x 6" (10cm x 15cm) contrast scrap for toe & heel caps, same fabrics as boots

NOTIONS:

Dress:
Two ⅜" (10mm) buttons (one should be decorative)

One package of ¼" (6mm) double-fold bias tape

2⅝ yds. (2.4m) of ⅛" (3mm) decorative cord

⅛ yd. (.2m) of ⅝" (15mm) Velcro® fastener tape

1½ yds. (1.4m) of ½" (1.3cm) soft ribbon

*Cut the neckband piece on the bias grainline.

Collar, Cuffs, Skirt Ruffle & Bloomer Ruffles:
3⅛ yds. (2.9m) of 2" (5cm) scalloped-edge lace

Bloomers:
⅝ yd. (.6m) of ¾" (20mm) single-edge scalloped edge lace trim

1 yd. (.4m) of ⅜" (10mm) elastic

Tights:
⅜ yd. (.4m) of ¼" (6mm) elastic

Boots:
5" x 3½" (12.5cm x 9cm) piece of medium-weight cardboard

½ yd. (.50m) of ¼" (6mm) ready-made piping

4" (10cm) of ¼" (6mm) Velcro® fastener tape

Eight (8) pearl ball buttons or pearls

SEE COLOR — CODED PIECES

MISCELLANEOUS:
Dressmaker's carbon paper, scissors, straight pins, craft glue, sewing needle

DRESS

Prepare the DRESS BODICE FRONT by marking the tucks with dressmaker's carbon paper. To fold the tucks, work on the right side of the fabric and bring the marked lines of the small •'s together. Sew along the stitching lines from the top edge to the bottom edge. Press the tucks away from the center front. Baste across the top and bottom edges to hold the tucks flat.

STEP

1

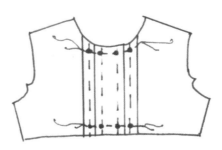

Cut four lengths of decorative cord the same length as each tuck. Center the cord over the stitching. Zigzag stitch directly over the stitching line of the tucks to attach the cord to the bodice.

STEP

2

With the right sides of the fabric together, stitch the DRESS BODICE BACKS to the bodice front at the shoulders. Press the seams toward the front. Fold the back opening edges to the inside along the fold line indicated on the pattern; press. Hand- or machine-baste across the upper and lower edges. Staystitch the neck edge to prevent stretching.

STEP

3

Cut two pieces of scalloped edge lace, each 6½" (16.5cm) long for the collar. Fold all but the scalloped edge to the wrong side ¼" (6mm). Hand-sew or zigzag stitch the edges in place. Run two rows of gathering stitches across the top of both pieces.

STEP

4

Mark the center of one DRESS NECKBAND piece. (Neckband pieces must be cut on the bias.) Gather the lace collar pieces to fit the neckband. Pin both collar sections to the neckband with the right sides together and notches matching; baste.

STEP 5

Press the seam allowance on the lower edge of the remaining neckband piece to the wrong side. With the rights sides of the fabric together, pin the neckband sections together with the collar pieces sandwiched between them. Stitch along the sides and upper edge. Trim the corners and all of the seam allowances to ⅛" (3mm). Turn the neckband right side out, extending the lace collars; gently press.

STEP 6

Pin the neckband to the bodice neck edge, matching the symbols and clipping the bodice neck edge up to the staystitching as needed. Stitch, keeping the pressed edge of the neckband free. Press the seam toward the neckband and collar. Fold the pressed edge of the neckband over the seam and slipstitch the neckband closed, concealing the seam.

STEP 7

To prepare the DRESS SLEEVES, mark and then fold the tucks by bringing the lines of the small •'s together. Stitch along the marked stitching lines. Press each tuck away from the center. Baste across the top and bottom raw edges. Center decorative cord over the stitching as on the bodice front. Using a zigzag stitch, sew the cording in place.

STEP 8

Gather the upper edge of the sleeves between the small •'s and gather the lower edge between the large •'s and seam allowances. Cut two pieces of 2" (5cm) lace, each 2½" (6.5cm) long. Position the wrong side of the lace trim on the right side of each CUFF, ¾" (2cm) down from the top edge, with the scalloped edge falling off the bottom edge of the cuff. Zigzag the lace to the cuff across the top of the lace; do not attach the lace at the scalloped edge.

STEP 9

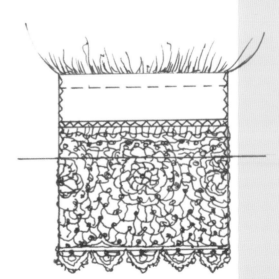

Fold the scalloped edge of the lace out of the way and sew the right side of the lower edge of the cuff to the right side of the lower edge of the sleeve. Do not catch the lace in the seam. Press the seam and fold the cuff down and the lace up and over the cuff seam; topstitch the lace in place directly over the cuff seam. Press under ¼" (6mm) along the unfinished edge of the cuff. Fold the cuff to the wrong side along the fold line; hand-sew the pressed edge of the cuff over the seam.

STEP
10

With the right sides of the fabric together, pin each sleeve to the bodice armhole edges, placing the large • at the shoulder seam. Adjust the sleeve gathers, so that the sleeve fits into the bodice smoothly; stitch. Press the seams toward the bodice.

STEP
11

With the right sides of the fabric together, pin the bodice front and bodice back together at the side seams and pin the sleeves together along the underarm. Stitch in one continuous seam; backstitch at the cuff and clip at the armhole. To neaten the cuff edge, press the seam allowances open and hand-sew the seam allowances flat.

STEP
12

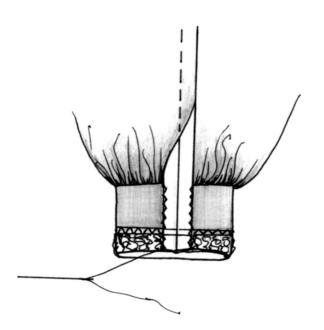

Clean finish the raw edges of the skirt back self-facing, which falls along the upper third of the DRESS SKIRT FRONT AND BACK. With the right sides of the fabric together, stitch the skirt front and back together, from the large • to the hem, leaving the back facing open. Turn the back self-facing to the inside along the fold line; press. Baste the top edges together by hand.

STEP
13

Clean finish the lower edge of the skirt. Turn up the hem along the marking and press. Baste the hem in place close to the fold. Hand-sew the hem. If you haven't already done so, transfer the tuck markings onto the skirt. Make the skirt tucks by bringing the lines of the small •'s together on the right side of the fabric. Sew along the stitching lines.

STEP 14

Center decorative cord over the placement line along the bottom of the skirt. Zigzag the cord in place. Pin the right side of the lace trim to the wrong side of the skirt, placing the unfinished edge of the lace slightly above the lower edge of the skirt and turning in the ends to meet at the center back. Baste, keeping the tucks free from the stitching. On the right side, zigzag along the basting, underneath the lowest tuck. Slipstitch the ends.

STEP 15

Gather the upper edge of the skirt between the small •'s. With the right sides of the fabric together, pin the skirt to the bodice, placing the small •'s at the side seams. Adjust the gathers so the pieces fit together and baste. Stitch and press the seam towards the bodice. Place decorative cord over the waist seam, turning the ends to the inside at the back opening edge. Zigzag stitch the cord in place directly over the seam edge.

STEP 16

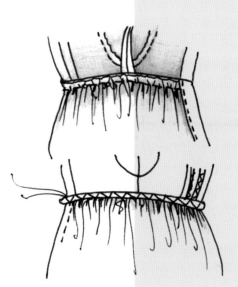

Cut one 3" (7.5cm)-long piece of velcro. Cut the piece in half lengthwise. Pin the stiffer loop section of the velcro to the outside of the right back opening along the edge. Extend the velcro ½" (1.3cm) beyond the waistline. Stitch it in place. Pin the softer loop section of the velcro to the left back opening edge on the inside of the dress; stitch it in place.

STEP 17

Sew a button to the right back neckband. Make a thread loop at the neck opening edge opposite the button and large enough for the button to pass through. Make a small ribbon bow with a small piece of ½" (1.3cm)-wide ribbon and tack it to the front neckband. Sew a decorative button over the front bow.

STEP 18

Loop the remaining ½" (1.3cm)-wide ribbon to form six loops with two streamers, one streamer on each side of the loops. Secure the loops together with a piece of thread. Tack the loops onto the left side of the dress back opening at the waist.

STEP 19

BLOOMERS

Turn up the hem on both BLOOMERS, turning in ¼" (6mm) on the raw edge; press. Stitch the hem close to the inner pressed edge. On the right side, pin the upper edge of lace trim ½" (1.3cm) below the stitching. Turn under the upper edge of the trim, if necessary to fit. To form a casing, stitch close to the upper edge of the trim. Stitch across the trim along the lower edge of the bloomers.

STEP 1

Cut two pieces of elastic, each the measurement of the upper leg of the doll, plus ½" (1.3cm). Insert the elastic into the casing, with raw edges even. Baste across the ends to hold the elastic in place.

STEP 2

With the right sides of the fabric together, stitch the bloomers together at the center front and center back. Stitch the inner leg edges together. To form the casing for the waist elastic, turn the upper edge to the inside along the fold line, turning under ¼" (6mm) on the raw edge; press. Stitch along the inner pressed edge, leaving a 2" (5cm) opening. Cut one piece of elastic the measurement of the doll's waist, plus ½" (1.3cm). Insert the elastic through the opening, lap the ends, and stitch them securely together. Push the elastic into the opening, smooth it and then stitch the opening closed while stretching the elastic slightly.

STEP 3

TIGHTS

STEP

1

Stretch the fabric slightly during stitching. With the right sides of the fabric together, sew the TIGHTS together at the center back and center front.

STEP

2

To form the casing for the waist elastic, turn the upper edge of the tights to the inside along the fold line; press it in place. Stitch close to the raw edge, leaving an opening. Cut one piece of elastic the measurement of the doll's waist, plus ½" (1.3cm).

STEP

3

Insert the elastic through the opening. Lap the ends of the elastic and stitch them together. Stitch the opening closed, stretching the elastic as you sew.

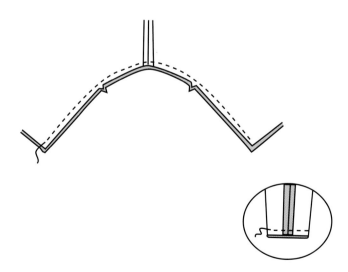

STEP

4

With the right sides of the fabric together, stitch the inner leg seam. To finish the bottom of the tights, fold the lower edges along the fold line, bring the small •'s together. Stitch across each lower edge.

BOOTS

Sew the left and right BOOT SIDE and BOOT SIDES AND BACK pieces with right sides together. Finger-press the seam allowances open, clipping the curve as necessary. Topstitch on the right side of the fabric along both sides of the seam.

STEP 1

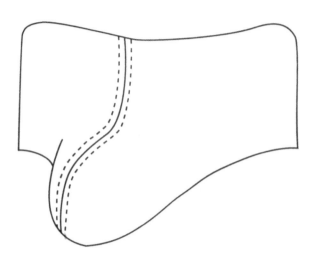

With the right sides of the fabric together, sew two of the TOE pieces and two of the HEEL pieces together along the curved, unnotched edges. Repeat with the remaining pieces. Trim the seam allowance of the heels to ⅛" (3mm). Turn the toe and heel sections right side out and press.

STEP 2

Topstitch the toes and heels to the boots. Add a second row of top-stitching. With the right sides together, sew piping to the top and sides of the boots in one continuous seam. Trim the boot fabric under the piping to ⅛" (3mm).

STEP 3

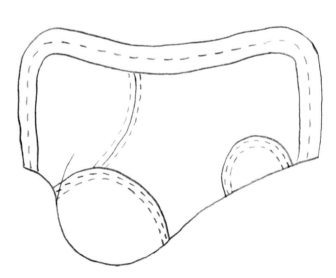

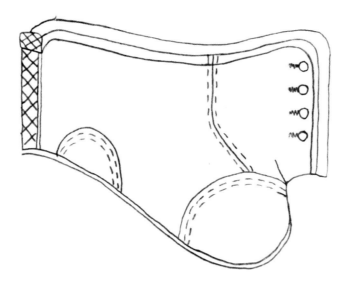

Press the piping up and the seam allowance to the wrong side of the boots. Topstitch the piping in place. Zigzag stitch four fake buttonholes to the right side of the boot. Machine- or hand-sew the stiffer loop section of a piece of velcro, cut the same length as the opening, under the piping and the buttonholes. Hand-sew the softer loop section of the velcro to the opposite side of the boot opening. Sew buttons directly over the stitched buttonholes.

STEP

4

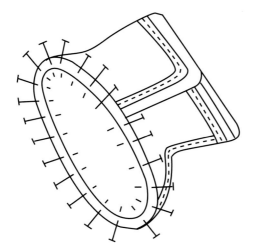

Close the boot tops. With the right sides of the fabric together, pin the BOOT BOTTOM to the bottom edge of the boot top. Use a generous supply of pins to ease the SOLE (bottom) in the opening. Sew the seam and trim it to ⅛" (3mm). Turn the boots right side out. Insert a cardboard sole in each boot, and glue them in place.

STEP

5

GENTLEMAN'S BEST

Essential garments for your boy doll: corduroy trousers, complete with suspenders, a handsome button-up shirt, and boots.

YOU WILL NEED:

FABRIC:

Shirt:
¼ yd. (.3m) of 45" (115cm)—cotton & cotton blends

Pants:
⅜ yd. (.4m) of 45" (115cm)—denim & corduroy

Loops & Tab:
5" x 3½" (13cm x 9cm)—synthetic leather remnant

Boots:
¼ yd. (.25m) or 7" x 12" (18cm x 30.5cm) scrap of linen, felt, ultrasuede, synthetic leather

NOTIONS:

Shirt:
Five ⁵⁄₁₆" (8mm) buttons

Five Size 3/0 snaps

Pants:
Six ⁵⁄₁₆" (8mm) buttons

Three Size 3/0 snaps

¾ yd. (.7m) of ⅝" (15mm) black elastic

Boots:
½ yd. (.50m) of ¼" (6mm) piping

4" (10cm) of ¼" (6mm) Velcro® fastener tape

5" x 3½" (12.5cm x 9cm) medium-weight cardboard

MISCELLANEOUS:

Dressmaker's carbon paper, scissors, straight pins, craft glue, sewing needle

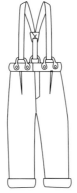

SEE COLOR — CODED PIECES

SHIRT

Make self-facings on the center front by pressing under ¼"
(6mm) along the raw edge of the SHIRT FRONT. Turn the
self-facing to the inside along the fold line and press. Stitch the
facings in place close to the inner pressed edges.

STEP

1

With the right sides
of the fabric together,
stitch the SHIRT
BACK to the front
sections at the
shoulders.

STEP

2

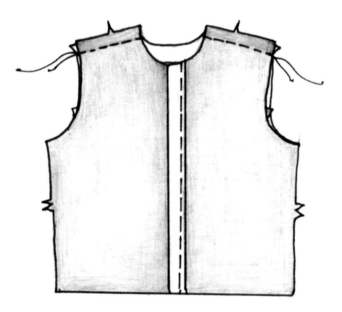

Staystitch the shirt neck edge to prevent the fabric from stretching. Finish the lower edge of one SHIRT COLLAR piece by
pressing the seam allowance to the inside. With the right sides
of the fabric together, stitch the two collar sections together,
pivoting at the small •'s. Leave the lower edge open. Clip to the
small •'s and trim the seam allowance. Turn the collar right side out and press.

STEP

3

With the right sides of the fabric together, pin the collar to the neck edge, clipping up to the staystitching at the neck edge of the garment to help the collar fit smoothly. Stitch the seam, taking care to keep the pressed edge free. Press the seam toward the collar. Fold the collar over the seam and slipstitch the pressed edge to cover the seam.

STEP
4

Gather the upper and lower edges of the SHIRT SLEEVES between the small •'s. Press the seam allowance along one long edge of each CUFF to the wrong side of the fabric. With the right sides of the fabric together, pin the cuff to the lower edge of the sleeve, adjusting the gathers. Stitch and press the seam toward the cuff. Turn the cuff to the inside along the fold line and slipstitch the pressed edge over the seam. Edgestitch along the upper edge of the cuff. Repeat with the remaining cuff and sleeve.

STEP
5

With the right sides of the fabric together, pin a sleeve to the armhole edge, placing the large • at the shoulder seam. Adjust the gathers. Stitch the seam and press the seam allowances toward the sleeve. Repeat with the remaining sleeve.

STEP
6

Again, with the right sides of the fabric together, pin the back and the front of the shirt together at the sides and sleeves. Stitch in one continuous seam. To hem the shirt, turn under ¼" (6mm) on the bottom edge and press. Turn up the hem ¼" (6mm) and stitch close to the upper edge of the pressed hem along the inside of the shirt.

STEP
7

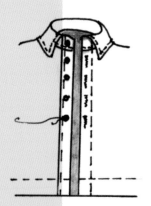

Make four buttonholes along the markings on the left front of the shirt. Do not cut the buttonholes open; instead, sew a button over each buttonhole and one on the collar at the button marking. Hand-sew the small ball sections of the snaps to the left front facing and collar under the buttons. Lap the left front over the right, aligning the centers of the shirt. Mark the placement of the snaps on the right front and collar and sew the socket sections of the snaps in place at the markings.

STEP

8

PANTS

The PANTS FRONT AND BACK are cut as one piece. Create a pleat on the right side of each piece by creasing along the line of the small •'s. Bring the folded creases to the line of the large •'s and baste. Baste across the upper waist edge as well; press. Stitch the darts and press them toward the center back.

STEP

1

With the right sides of the fabric together, stitch the inner leg crotch seam below the small •. Clip the front seam allowances below the fly extension. Turn in the seam allowance on the extensions and press. Stitch the right front seam allowance in place. Fold the left front extension to the inside along the fold line and baste it in place. On the right side of the fabric, stitch the left front extension along the stitching line, keeping the front extension free.

STEP

2

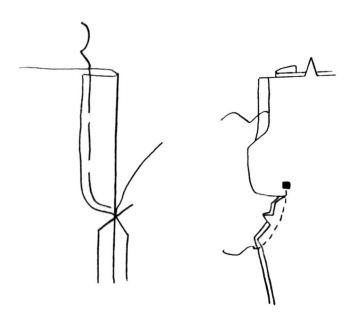

With the right sides of the fabric together, stitch the inner leg edges (inseam) of the front and back in one continuous seam. Clip the seam.

STEP 3

Press under the seam allowance along one long, unnotched edge of the PANTS WAISTBAND. Pin the waistband to the upper edge of the pants with the right sides of the fabric together and the notches matching; stitch. Press the seam toward the waistband.

STEP 4

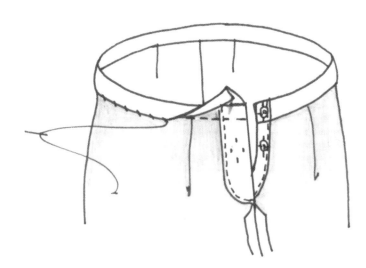

Fold the waistband along the fold line so that the right sides of the fabric are together and stitch the short ends. Turn the waistband right side out, fold it over the seam, and press it in place. Slipstitch the waistband closed, encasing the seam. Sew two snaps to the waistband and one on the front opening at the small •'s.

STEP 5

Fold the pant leg hems to the inside along the markings and baste close to the fold. Trim the hems to an even width if necessary. Finish the raw edges with pinking shears, a serger, or a machine zigzag stitch, and hand-sew the hems. Fold the lower edge of the fabric to the right side to make cuffs. Press or hand-tack the cuffs in place at the inseam.

STEP 6

Cut out one TAB and three PANTS SUSPENDERS pieces from the synthetic leather and transfer all the markings. To make the suspender loops, fold the three long pieces in half lengthwise with the wrong sides of the fabric together. Apply glue to the center of the fold and leave the ends flat. Let the glue dry. Place the loops on the waistband, matching the small squares. Sew one button at each square through all the thicknesses.

STEP 7

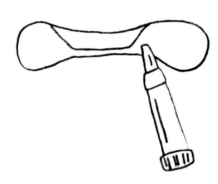

STEP 8

To make the suspender straps, cut one piece of elastic 23" (58.5cm) long. Stitch along the open, long edge. Insert the elastic through the back loop and pull it until the ends are even. Baste the elastic together 2" (5cm) above the loop. Place the remaining suspender section over the elastic at the basting mark. Gently pull the elastic to separate it at the upper edge forming a 'V'. Stitch the tab in place, close to all the edges.

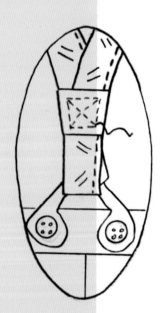

STEP 9

Put the pants on the doll to mark the correct length of the suspenders. Thread the ends of the braid through the front loops from front to back. Pin the ends of braid in place so that the suspenders are taut, but not tight. Take the pants off the doll, leaving the pins in place. Trim the ends if necessary. Stitch the ends securely to form the suspenders.

BOOTS

Note: Use boot pattern pieces from Festive Finery.

Sew the left and right BOOT SIDE and BOOT SIDE AND BACK pieces with right sides together. Finger-press the seam allowances open, clipping the curve as necessary. Topstitch on the right side of the fabric along both sides of the seam.

STEP 1

With the right sides together, sew piping to the top and sides of the boots in one continuous seam. Trim the boot fabric under the piping to ⅛" (3mm).

STEP 2

Press the piping up and the seam allowance to the wrong side of the boots. Topstitch the piping in place. Hand-sew the stiffer looped section of a piece of velcro, cut the same length as the opening, under the piping. Hand-sew the softer loop section of the velcro to the opposite side of the boot opening.

STEP 3

Close the boot tops. With the right sides of the fabric together, pin the BOOT BOTTOM pieces to the bottom edge of the boot tops. Use a generous supply of pins to ease the sole in the opening. Sew the seam and trim it to ⅛" (3mm). Turn the boots right side out. Insert a cardboard SOLE (bottom) in each boot. Glue the cardboard in place.

STEP 4

CLOAKED IN COMFORT

Dress your doll in a vintage-style cape and hat that harks back to the romance of a bygone era.

YOU WILL NEED:

FABRIC:

Cape & Hat:
¼ yd. (.7m) of 45" (115cm) fabric—wool, wool blends, crepe (Note: The wrong side of the fabric does show.)

NOTIONS:

Cape & Hat:

1⅜ yds. (1.5m) of ⅜" (10mm) ribbon

1½ yds. (1.4m) of ⅝" (15mm) ribbon

3 yds. (2.8m) of ³⁄₁₆" (5mm) decorative cording

MISCELLANEOUS:

Dressmaker's carbon paper, scissors, straight pins

To make a perfect 1/4 circle with a radius of 23" (58.5cm), cut a piece of fabric 23" (58.5cm) square on the straight grain. Plot the radius from one corner using a ruler or piece of string. By holding the ruler or string at the corner and marking 23" (58.5cm) at various points across the opposite edge, you create a perfect circle shape. Cut away the excess fabric along the marking.

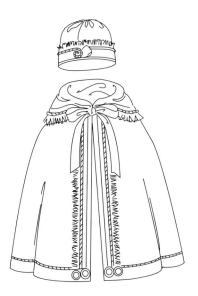

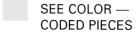

SEE COLOR — CODED PIECES

CAPE

Refer to the pattern information on page 131 and draw the CAPE pattern using the schematic drawing and cut a quarter circle with a 23" (58.5cm) radius. Transfer markings. The straight edges of the cape must be on the straight grain of the fabric for it to fringe.

STEP 1

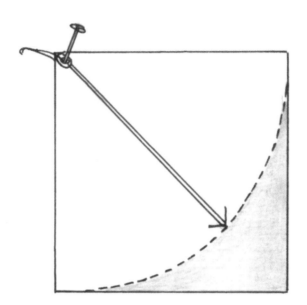

Fringe the side edges of the cape by sewing with very small stitches along the indicated stitching line, pivoting at the small •. Remove the lengthwise and crosswise threads from the raw edges up to the stitching line.

STEP 2

Sew ⅜" (1cm) ribbon to the wrong side of the cape over the placement line. Miter the ribbon at the corner.

STEP 3

Prepare the CASING for the back of the cape by pressing the short edges to the wrong side of the fabric along the fold lines and the long edges to the wrong side of the fabric along the seam allowances.

STEP 4

On the right side of the CAPE, pin the casing between the placement lines, matching the small •'s. Edgestitch the casing along the long edges, leaving the short ends open.

STEP
5

Make a ¼" (2cm) clip into the lower edge of the cape along the fold lines at each side front. Do not hem from the fold lines to the fringed edge at this point. Press the lower, curved edge under ¼" (6mm). Run a gathering stitch along the folded edge. Pull the gathering stitch to help the curved edge lay flat and press the edge under ½" (1.3cm). Stitch the hem in place.

STEP
6

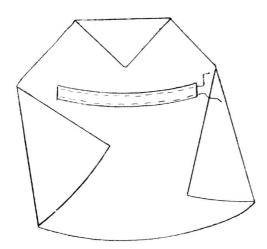

Press under ¼" (6mm) along the remaining lower edge. Turn the fringed edges to the right side along the fold line and the lower edges to the inside. Hand-sew the remaing hem edges. Stitch directly over the ribbon trim, up to the square marking near the casing to hold the fringed edge to the right side.

STEP
7

Hand-sew or machine sew with a zigzag stitch decorative cording to the right side of the cape, ½" (1.3cm) from the bottom edge and to the left of the ribbon along each fringed edge. Form double loops at the lower corners.

STEP
8

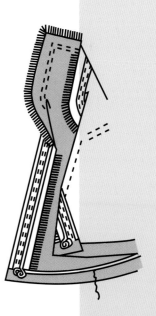

Make a bow from the remaining ⅜" (1cm) ribbon; trim the ends diagonally. Tack the bow to the corner of the cape at the small •, as shown.

STEP

9

HAT

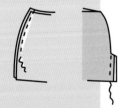

Set the machine stitch length to very small stitches and stitch along the indicated stitching line on the lower edge of the HAT. Fringe the lower edge by carefully pulling out the lengthwise threads from the raw edge up to the stitching line.

STEP

1

Pin ⅝" (15mm) ribbon to the lower edge of the hat, centering the ribbon over the placement line. Stitch the ribbon along both long edges, looping one end over the other.

STEP 2

Stitch the dart in the hat and press it open. With the right sides of the fabric together, stitch the center front edges of the hat together above the large •. Clip to, but not through, the large •. Turn the hat right side out and with wrong sides together, stitch the remainder of the center front seam below the large •. Gather the upper edge of the hat between the small •'s.

STEP 3

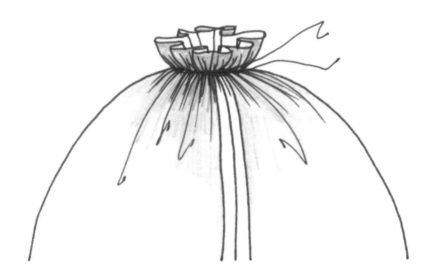

Turn the lower edge of the hat from the wrong side to the right side along the fold lines and press. The wrong side of the fabric shows. Hand-sew or machine sew with a zigzag stitch decorative cording to the hat along the upper edge of the ribbon, forming a loop over the looped end of the ribbon. On the inside of the hat, pull the gathering threads tightly to shape the hat. Knot the thread ends securely. Turn the hat right side out.

STEP 4

LOVELY LINGERIE

Ultra-feminine foundation pieces for the well-dressed doll: a camisole, petticoat, and bloomers.

YOU WILL NEED:

FABRIC:

Camisole, Petticoat & Bloomers:

⅝ yd. (.6m) of 45" (115cm) fabric—cotton, batiste, cotton blends

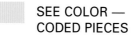
SEE COLOR —
CODED PIECES

NOTIONS:

Camisole, Petticoat & Bloomers:

⅛ yd. (.2m) of ⅝" (15mm) beading trim

2½ yds. (2.3m) of ⅞" (22mm) pregathered lace with beading trim*

3¼ yds. (3.0m) of ⅛" (3mm) satin ribbon

⅞ yd. (.8m) of ¼" (6mm) elastic

¾ yd. (.7m) of 2" (50mm) lace ruffling

⅛ yd. (.2m) of ⅝" (15mm) Velcro® fastener tape

*If you can't find pregathered lace with beading trim, buy pregathered lace and beading trim separately and sew them together. Treat them as one trim.

MISCELLANEOUS:

Dressmaker's carbon paper, scissors, straight pins

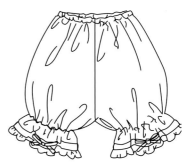

CAMISOLE

STEP

1

Make two tucks down the center of each CAMISOLE FRONT by bringing the small •'s together on the right side of the fabric. Stitch and then press the tucks toward the side. Turn the front extension to the inside along the fold line, folding under ¼" (6mm) on the raw edge; press. Stitch close to the inner folded edge. Baste the upper and lower edges in place.

STEP

2

With the right sides of the fabric together, stitch the camisole front and CAMISOLE BACK together at the shoulders. Turn the neck and armhole edges to the right side of the fabric along the seamlines. Clip the seam allowance periodically so it lays flat; press.

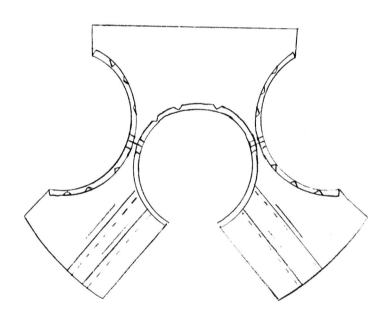

On the right side of the camisole, pin the flat beaded trim along the right edge of the center front. Baste the long edges in place. Pin the pregathered lace and beaded trim to the neck and armhole edges, covering the seam allowances. Turn under ¼" (6mm) on the short ends of the neck trim so that the ends line up with the finished edges of the camisole front. Stitch close to the long edges and across the short ends of all the trim through all the thicknesses.

STEP

3

With the right sides of the fabric together, stitch the front to the back at the sides. Fold the lower edge of the camisole to the right side of the fabric along the seamline; press. Pin the pregathered lace and beaded trim to the lower edge, over the seam allowances, turning under ¼" (6mm) on the short ends so they line up with the finished front edges. Stitch close to the straight edges, through all the thicknesses.

STEP 4

Stitch the stiffer loop section of the velcro onto the wrong of the right front opening, close to the outer edge. Stitch the softer loop section onto the right side of the left front opening, close to the outer edge. Cut two 5" (12.5cm) pieces of ⅛" (3mm) satin ribbon. Tie each piece into a bow and trim the ends diagonally. Tack the bows to the upper and lower edges of the right front.

STEP 5

PETTICOAT

Fold ¼" (6mm) to the wrong side on the lower edge of the PETTICOAT. Fold an additional ¼" (6mm) to the wrong side to clean finish the raw edge; press. Baste close to the inner edge. To make the tucks, bring the lines of the small •'s together on the right side of the fabric and stitch. Press the tucks toward the hem.

STEP 1

To form the waistline casing, turn the upper edge of the petticoat to the inside along the fold line, turning under ¼" (6mm) on the raw edge. Press, and stitch close to the inner edge. Cut a 9½" (24cm) piece of elastic. Insert the elastic into the casing so that the elastic ends are even with the raw edges of the petticoat. Baste the ends to secure the elastic.

STEP 2

On the right side of the petticoat, pin the pregathered lace ruffling to the lower edge so that the bound edge of the trim covers the lower edge; stitch. With the right sides of the fabric together, stitch the center back seam.

STEP

3

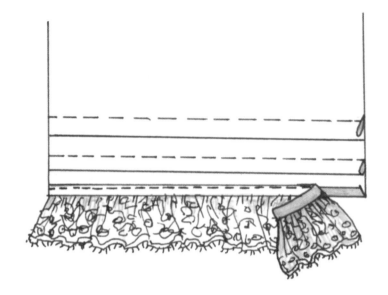

To finish the petticoat, pin the pregathered lace with beaded trim over the bound edge of the lace ruffling, and turn the short ends under so they meet at the center back. Stitch the trim close to both long edges of the beading. Slipstitch the ends in place.

STEP

4

BLOOMERS

Press ¼" (6mm) to the right side of the fabric along the lower edge of the BLOOMERS. Pin the pregathered lace with beaded trim over the pressed edge. Stitch close to both long edges of the trim. Cut two 6" (15cm) lengths of elastic. Sew one piece of elastic to each lower leg edge by centering it over the placement line and stretching it to fit.

STEP

1

With the right sides of the fabric together, stitch the bloomers at the center front, the center back, and then at the inner leg seam.

STEP
2

To form the waist casing, turn the upper edge of the fabric to the inside along the fold line, turning under ¼" (6mm) on the raw edge; press. Stitch close to the inner edge, leaving a small opening to insert the elastic.

STEP
3

Cut a 9½" (24cm) piece of elastic. Insert the elastic into the casing. Lap the ends and stitch them securely. Smooth the elastic into the casing and stitch the opening closed, stretching the elastic while stitching.

STEP
4

Cut two 5" (12.5cm) pieces of satin ribbon. Tie each piece into a bow and trim the ends diagonally. Tack the bows in place through all the thicknesses.

STEP
5

MODERN MISS

Perfect for school or playtime, this easy-going ensemble includes fun mix-and-match pieces.

YOU WILL NEED:

FABRIC:

Dress & Hat:
⅜ yd. (.5m) of 45" (115cm) fabric—moderate stretch knits only

Tights:
⅜ yd. (.5m) of 45" (115cm) fabric—moderate stretch knits only

Vest:
¼ yd. (.3m) of 45" (115cm) fabric—cotton broadcloth, flannel, denim, chambray, lightweight woolens

¼ yd. (.3m) of 45" (115cm) lining fabric

NOTIONS:

Dress:
One ½" (1.3cm) flat button

⅛ yd. (.3m) of ⅝" (15mm) Velcro® fastener tape

Vest:
One 6" (15cm) separating metal jeans zipper

One ½" (13mm) button

⅛ yd. (.3m) of ⅝" (15mm) Velcro® fastener tape

Seam binding

Tights:
⅜ yd. (.4m) of ½" (1.3cm) elastic

MISCELLANEOUS:

Dressmaker's carbon paper, scissors, straight pins

SEE COLOR —
CODED PIECES

DRESS

Prevent the shoulders from stretching by basting seam binding over the center of the seamline on the right shoulders of both the DRESS FRONT and DRESS BACK pieces. With the right sides of the fabric together, stitch the back to the front at the right shoulder seam. Press the left front and back shoulder seam to the wrong side of the fabric along the fold lines.

Topstitch the front and back along the left shoulder. Press the seam allowance to the wrong side of the fabric along the long, unnotched edge of the DRESS NECKBAND. Fold the neckband along the fold line so that the right sides of the fabric are together. Stitch the short ends. Turn the band right side out and press.

Pin the neckband to the garment with the right sides of the fabric together,

matching the symbols and clipping the seam allowances as necessary for a smooth fit. Stitch the seam, keeping the pressed edge of the band free. Press the seam toward the neckband. Slipstitch the pressed edge over the seam.

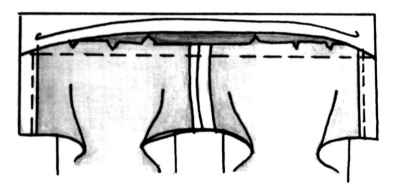

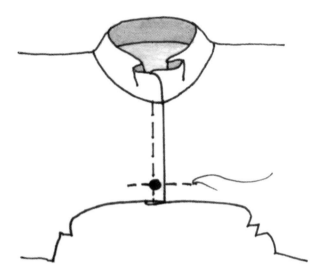

Lap the left front shoulder over the left back shoulder, matching the symbols. Baste the edges together along the armhole edge.

STEP 4

Easestitch the upper edge of each sleeve between the notches. Press each SLEEVE hem to the wrong side of the fabric and stitch close to the raw edge. With the right sides of the fabric together, pin each sleeve to an armhole edge, matching the large • to the shoulder seam. Adjust the ease and stitch the seam. Press the seam toward the sleeve.

STEP 5

With the right sides of the fabric together, stitch the side and sleeve edges together in one continuous seam. Fold the lower hem edge to the wrong side of the garment and press. Stitch the hem close to the raw edge.

STEP 6

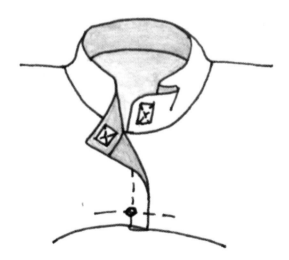

Cut one ½" (1.3cm) square of velcro. Pin the stiffer loop section to the outside, back edge of the neckband opening and the softer loop section to the inside front edge of the neckband opening; stitch them in place. Sew the button on the right side of the neckband at the marking.

STEP 7

HAT

With the right sides
of the fabric together,
stitch the upper
curved edge of the
HAT, ending at the
small •. Clip to the small •.

STEP

1

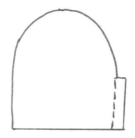

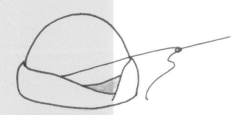

Turn the hat right side out and press. Stitch the remainder of the
seam below the small • with the wrong side of the fabric together.
To form the brim, turn up 1" (2.5cm) on the lower edge of the
hat. Turn up the lower edge again 1½" (3.8cm). Tack the brim to
the hat at the seams.

STEP

2

TIGHTS

With the right sides of the fabric together, stitch the TIGHTS
FRONT AND BACK pieces together at the center front and the
center back. Stretch the fabric slightly during stitching.

STEP

1

To form the waistline casing, press the upper edge to the inside
along the fold line. Stitch close to the raw edge, leaving a small
opening for the elastic. Cut a 10" (25.5cm) piece of elastic and
insert it through the opening into the casing. Lap the ends of the
elastic and stitch them together.

STEP

2

Stitch the opening closed, stretching the elastic as you stitch. With
the right sides of the fabric together, stitch the inner leg seam. To
finish the bottom of the tights, fold the legs along the fold lines,
bring the small •'s together. Stitch across the lower edge.

STEP

3

VEST

Press the seam allowances along the front opening edges to the wrong side of the fabric on the VEST FRONT AND BACK piece. Open the zipper. Pin each zipper section right side up under the front opening edges, centering the zipper between the upper and lower seamlines. Hand-baste each zipper section in place. Use a zipper foot to edgestitch along the front opening, catching the zipper tape in the stitching. Remove the basting.

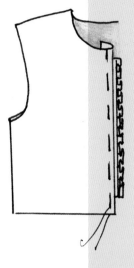

Press the seam allowances of the front and back lining to the wrong side along the front opening and the shoulder edges. With the right sides of the fabric and the lining together, pin the lining to the front and back of the vest with the raw edges even. Stitch the neck, armhole, and lower edges together.

Turn the lining to the inside and press. Slipstitch the front opening edges of the lining to the zipper tape. At each shoulder seam, slipstitch the lined edges together.

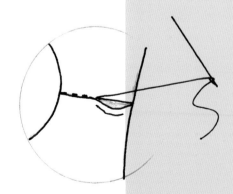

SLEEPING IN STYLE

Nightclothes are important for any child's doll. Dress the doll in this retro-style bonnet and gown, then tuck dolly in goodnight.

YOU WILL NEED:

FABRIC:

Nightshirt & Cap:
⅞ yd. (.8m) of 45" (115cm) fabric

NOTIONS:

Nightshirt:
⅞ yd. (.8m) of 1" (25mm) flat lace
⅜ yd. (.4m) of ¼" (6mm) middy braid
⅜ yd. (.4m) of ⅛" (3mm) cord
¼ yd. (.3m) of ¼" (6mm) elastic
Package of ¼" (6mm) white piping
Snap

Cap:
½ yd. (0.5m) fusible interfacing,
⅜ yd. (0.4m) of 1" (25mm) flat lace
⅞ yd. (0.8m) of ½" (13mm) ribbon

MISCELLANEOUS:

Dressmaker's carbon paper, scissors, straight pins

SEE COLOR —
CODED PIECES

NIGHTSHIRT

Working on the right side of the fabric, make the tucks on the NIGHTSHIRT FRONT by bringing the lines of the small •'s together. Stitch along the tuck markings; backstitch at the small •'s at the lower end of each tuck. Press the tucks away from the center front so that two tucks are pressed toward one side seam and the remaining tucks are pressed toward the opposite side seam. To hold the tucks in place, baste across the upper edge.

STEP 1

Position flat lace along the center front between the tucks. Stitch from the neck down to the hem on each side of the lace. Baste across each short end.

STEP 2

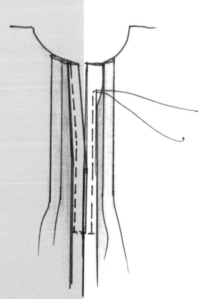

Make the tucks on each NIGHTSHIRT BACK piece just like the front tucks in step one. With the right sides of the fabric together, stitch the center back seam from the small • down to the hem. Leave the seam open above the small • and clean finish each raw edge with a narrow hem. To make a narrow hem, press ¼" (6mm) under and then ¼" (6mm) again; stitch close to the folded edge, pivoting across the seam allowance ¼" (6mm) below the small •.

STEP 3

With the right sides of the fabric together, stitch the back sections to the front at the shoulders.

STEP
4

Cut two pieces of piping to fit around the outer edge of the collar pieces. Pin one of the pieces of piping to the right side of one COLLAR section, placing the ridge of the piping just inside the seamline. Baste the piping in place, close to the ridge with a zipper foot. Repeat with the remaining piece of piping and one more collar section. With the right sides of the fabric together, pin the remaining collar sections to the collars with piping. Stitch, again with a zipper foot, leaving the neck edge open. Trim the seam allowances and turn the collars right side out; press. Baste the raw edges of each collar together.

STEP
5

With the right sides of the fabric together, pin the two collars to the upper edge of one of the COLLAR BANDS, matching the symbols and clipping the collar wherever it's necessary so that the collar pieces fit; baste.

STEP
6

Turn and press under the seam allowance along the lower edge of the remaining collar band, ease the fullness wherever it is necessary. With the right sides of the fabric together and the collars caught between, pin the collar band sections together. Stitch across the short ends and upper edge as shown. Leave the lower edge open. Turn the collar bands right side out and press.

STEP
7

With the right sides of the fabric together, pin the collar band to the neck edge of the garment, matching the symbols. Stitch, keeping the pressed edge of the remaining collar band free. Press the seam toward the collar band, clipping the seam allowance as needed for the collar band to turn smoothly. Slipstitch the pressed edge of the collar band over the seam.

STEP

8

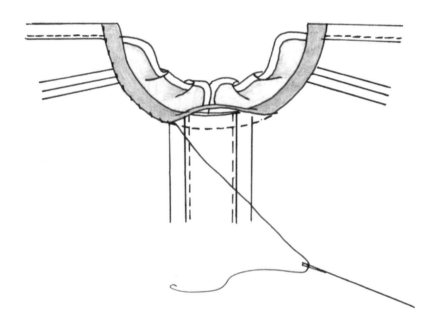

Edgestitch around the entire collar band, both upper and lower edges and across the short ends.

STEP

9

Center a piece of flat lace over the placement lines on each sleeve. Stitch close to each long edge, always starting from the same side so the stitching is done in the same direction each time. Baste across the short ends. Gather the upper edge of each NIGHTSHIRT SLEEVE between the notches with two rows of gathering stitches.

STEP

10

Press under ¼" (6mm) along the lower edge of each sleeve. Fold the lower edge to the inside of the fabric along the fold line and press. Stitch close to the inner pressed edge. To create a casing, stitch ⅜" (10mm) away from the previous stitching. Cut two pieces of elastic, each 3½" (9cm) long. Insert one of the elastic lengths into the casing and pull it so that the ends are even. Baste across the ends to secure the elastic.

STEP

11

With the right sides of the fabric together, pin each sleeve to an armhole edge, placing the large • at the shoulder seam. Adjust and smooth the gathers and baste. Check that the gathers look good from the right side and stitch the seam. Press the seam toward the garment.

STEP 12

Sew the front and back together in one continuous seam from the sleeve edge to the hem, with right sides of the fabric together. Press the seams. Tack the seam allowances down at the sleeve hem.

STEP 13

Gather the upper edge of the NIGHTSHIRT RUFFLE with two rows of gathering stitches. With the right sides of the ruffle together, stitch the short ends. Sew a ½" (1.3cm) narrow hem on the lower edge of the ruffle.

STEP 14

Pin the ruffle to the lower edge of the garment with the right sides of the fabric together and the small •'s at the side seams. Adjust the gathers and baste the ruffle in place. Stitch the seam and then press it toward the garment.

STEP 15

Sew a snap to the collar band. Tie middy braid into a bow and trim the ends diagonally. Tack the bow onto the collar band at the left back neck opening.

STEP 16

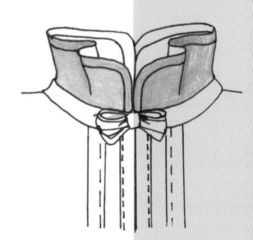

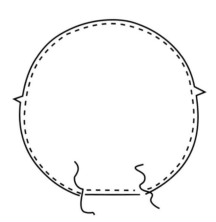

CAP

Fuse interfacing to the wrong side of both CAP BRIM pieces, following manufacturer's instructions. Reinforce the inner corners of the CAP CROWN by stitching along the seam allowance, pivoting at the large •'s. Clip diagonally into the large •'s.

Fold the seam allowance on the side edges of the crown to the wrong side below the large • and press. Make a ⅝" (15mm) narrow hem on the lower edge between the large •'s. Gather all around the outer edge of the crown between the large •'s.

Pin flat lace to the right side of the brim, centering it over the placement line. Stitch close to both long edges, always stitching in the same direction. Baste across the short ends.

Press the seam allowance along the long, unnotched edge of the brim to the wrong side. Fold the brim along the fold line so that the right sides of the fabric are together. Stitch the short ends together. Turn the brim right side out.

STEP 4

With the right side of the fabric together, pin the brim to the crown, matching the symbols. Adjust the gathers and baste the pieces together. Check that the gathers are even from the right side and then stitch the seam, keeping the pressed edge free. Press the seam toward the brim. Slipstitch the pressed edge of the brim over the seam, enclosing the seam for a neat finish.

STEP 5

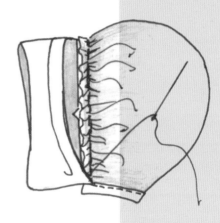

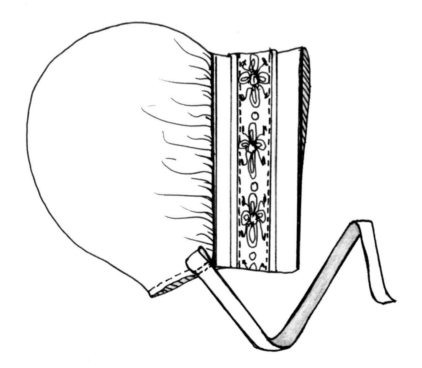

Cut two pieces of ribbon, each 14" (36cm) long. Press one end of each length of ribbon ½" (1.3cm) to the wrong side. Tack the pressed edge of the ribbon to the brim and trim the remaining ends diagonally.

STEP 6

Note: For patterns in photograph other than cape, see Vogue Pattern #8337.

PATTERNS

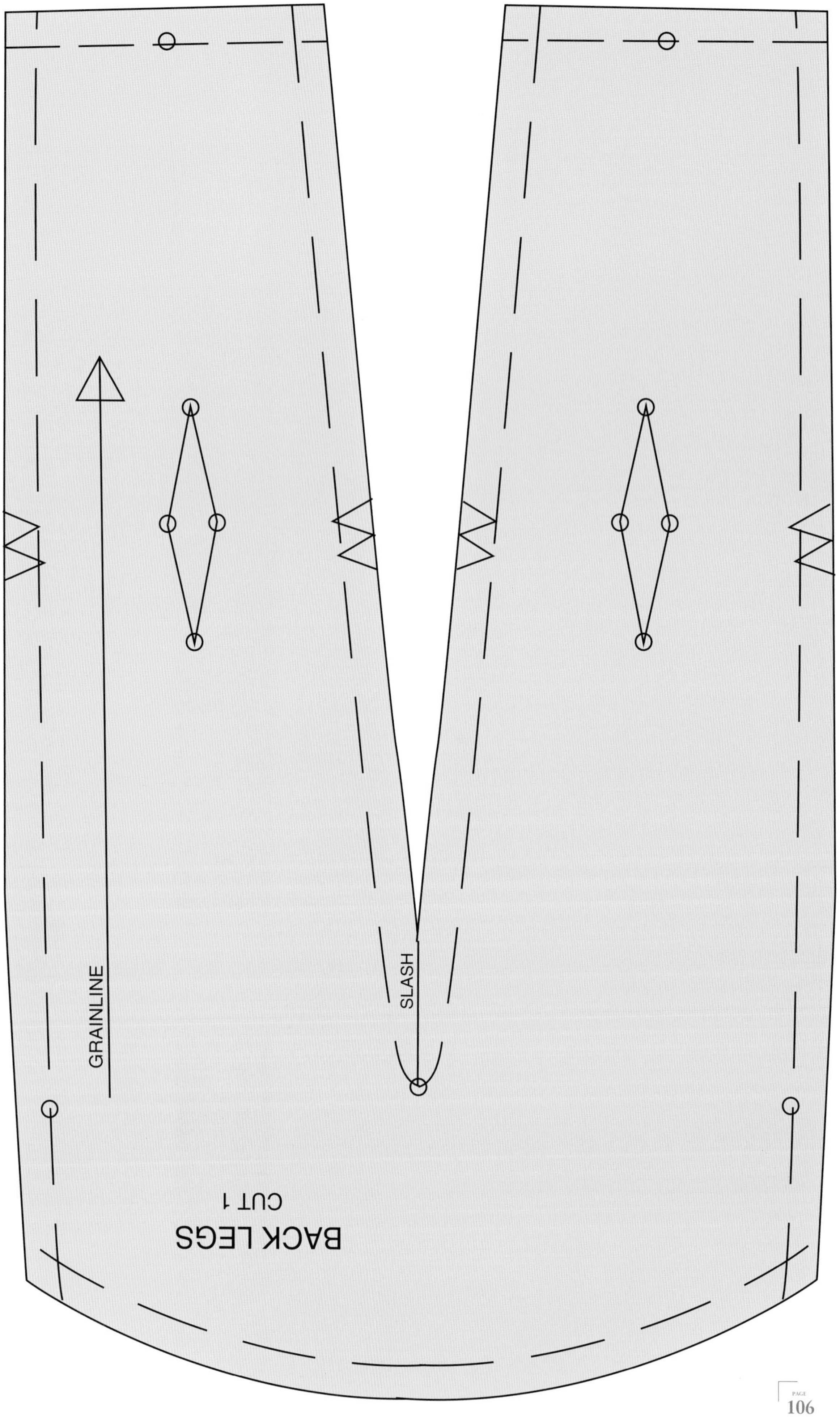

GRAINLINE

SLASH

BACK LEGS
CUT 1

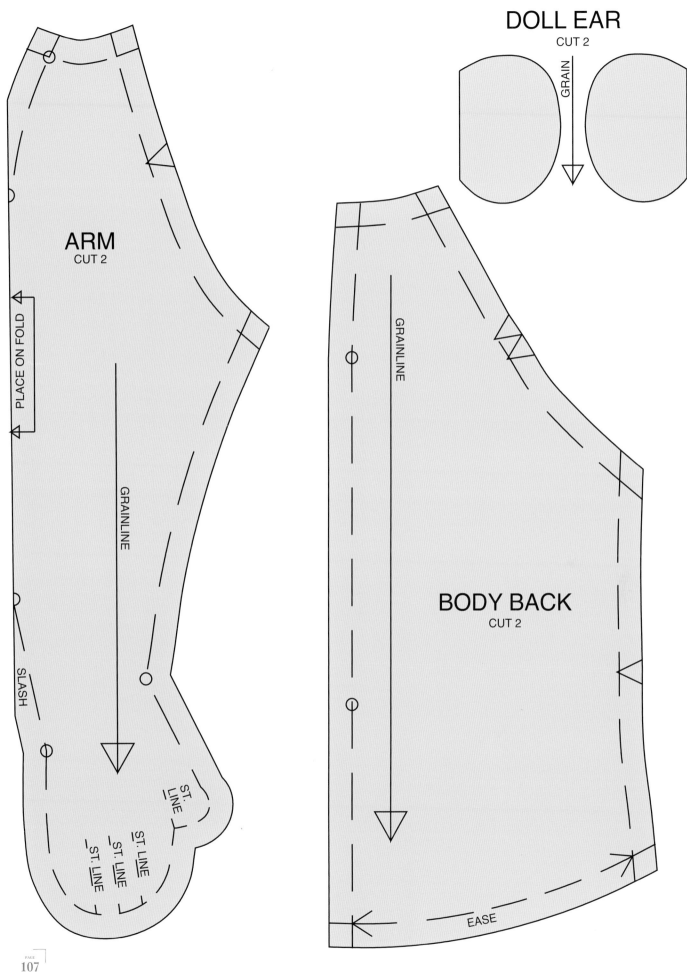

DOLL EAR

CUT 2

GRAIN

ARM

CUT 2

PLACE NO FOLD

GRAINLINE

SLASH

ST. LINE

ST. LINE

ST. LINE

ST. LINE

GRAINLINE

BODY BACK

CUT 2

EASE

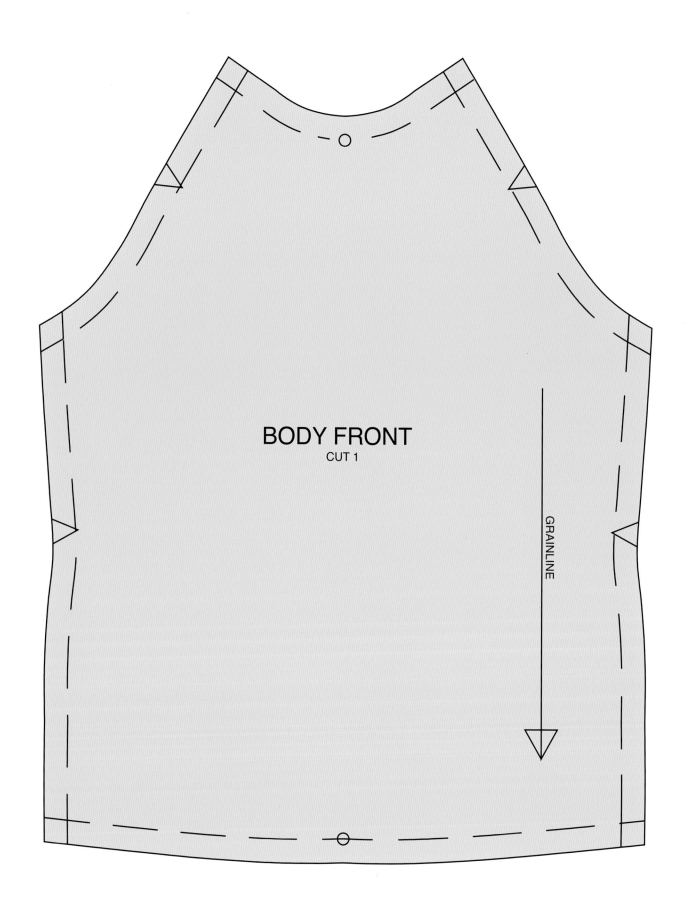

BODY FRONT

CUT 1

GRAINLINE

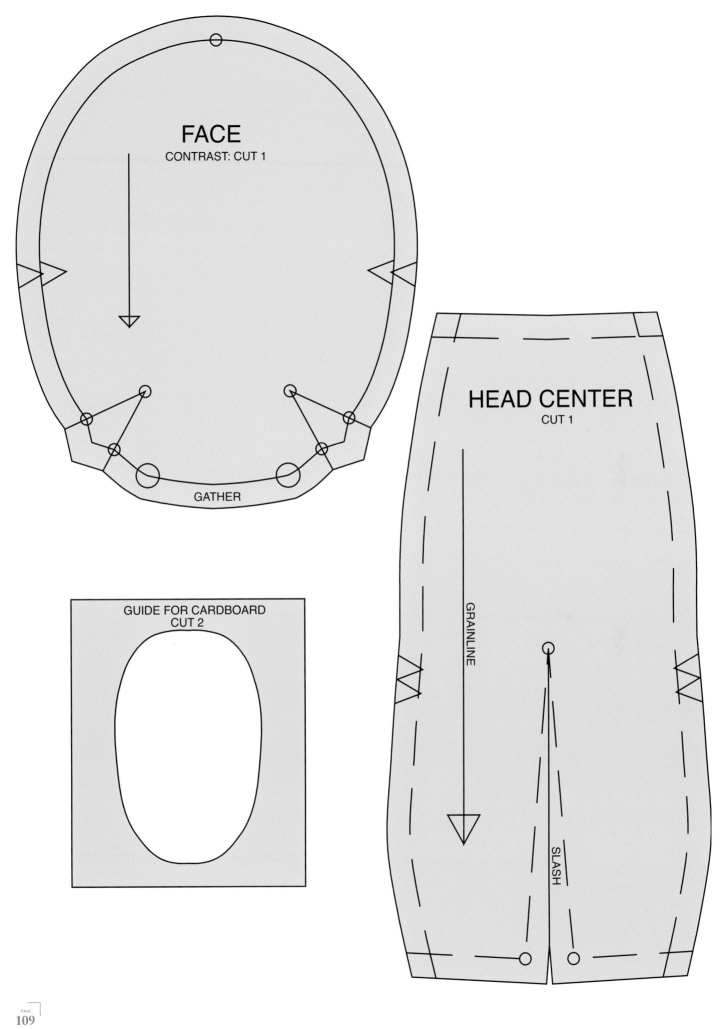

FACE
CONTRAST: CUT 1

HEAD CENTER
CUT 1

GRAINLINE

SLASH

GATHER

GUIDE FOR CARDBOARD
CUT 2

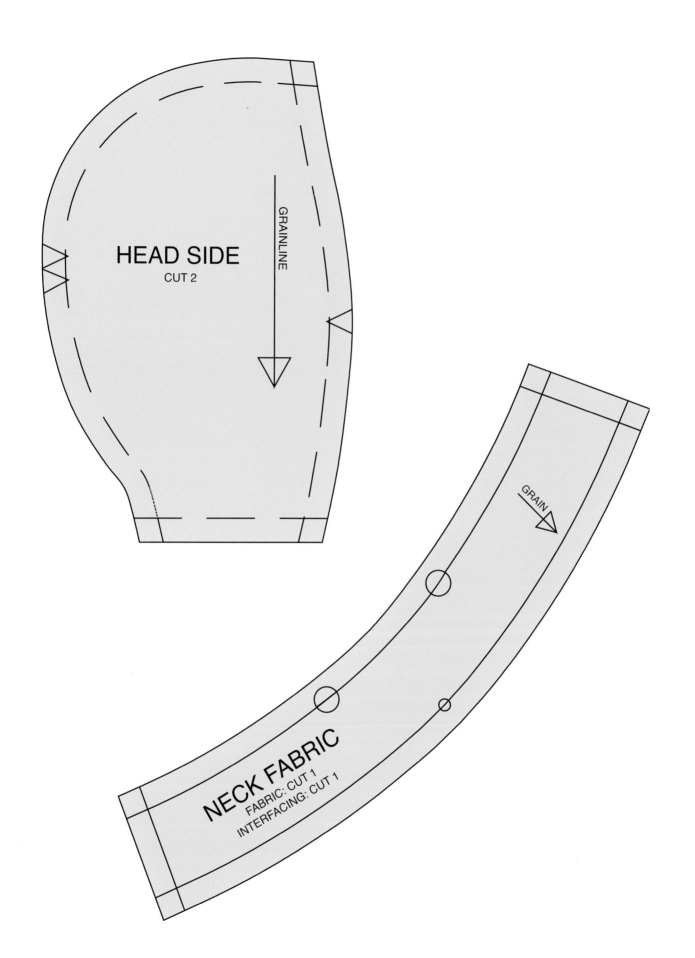

HEAD SIDE

CUT 2

GRAINLINE

NECK FABRIC

FABRIC: CUT 1

INTERFACING: CUT 1

GRAIN

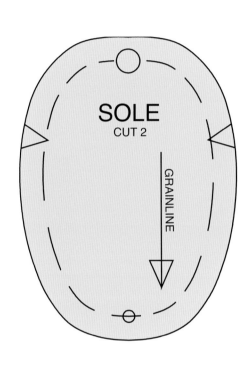

SOLE
CUT 2

GRAINLINE

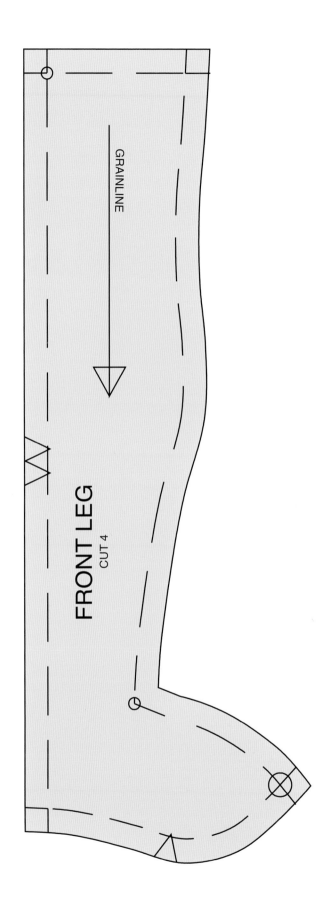

GRAINLINE

FRONT LEG
CUT 4

GRAINLINE

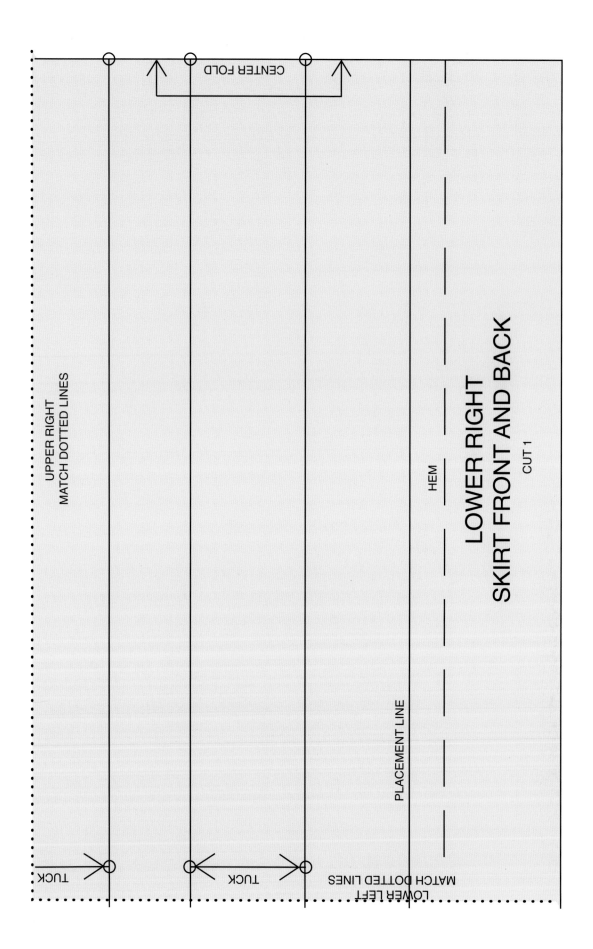

UPPER RIGHT
MATCH DOTTED LINES

CENTER FOLD

LOWER RIGHT
SKIRT FRONT AND BACK
CUT 1

HEM

PLACEMENT LINE

TUCK

TUCK

LOWER LEFT
MATCH DOTTED LINES

CENTER FOLD

GATHER

UPPER RIGHT
SKIRT FRONT AND BACK
CUT 1

LOWER RIGHT
MATCH DOTTED LINES

UPPER LEFT
MATCH DOTTED LINES

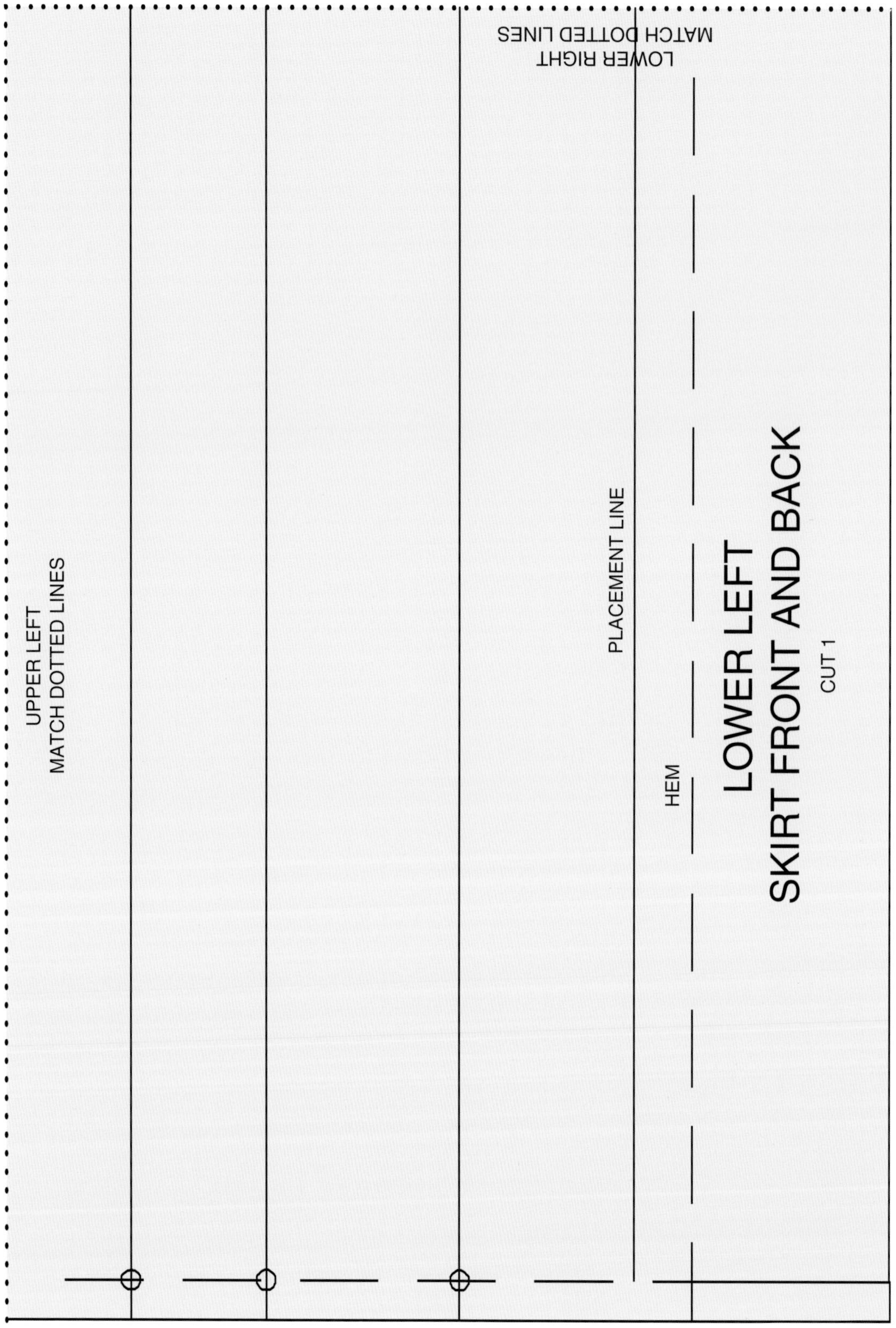

UPPER LEFT
MATCH DOTTED LINES

LOWER RIGHT
MATCH DOTTED LINES

PLACEMENT LINE

HEM

LOWER LEFT
SKIRT FRONT AND BACK
CUT 1

UPPER RIGHT
MATCH DOTTED LINES

GATHER

UPPER LEFT
SKIRT FRONT AND BACK
CUT 1

LOWER LEFT
MATCH DOTTED LINES

FOLDLINE (LEFT SIDE)

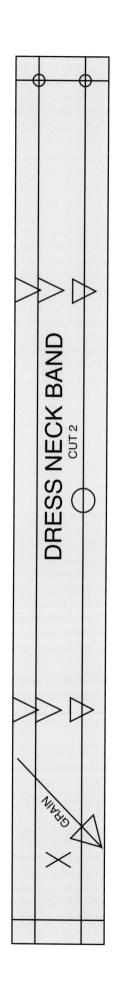

DRESS NECK BAND

CUT 2

GRAIN

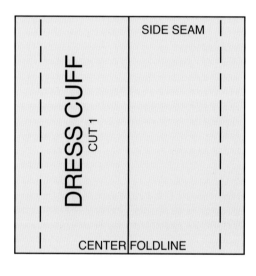

DRESS CUFF

CUT 1

SIDE SEAM

CENTER FOLDLINE

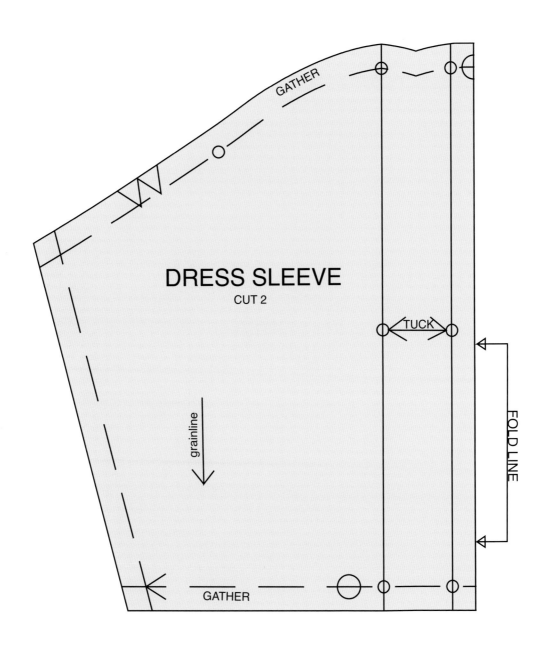

GATHER

DRESS SLEEVE

CUT 2

grainline

TUCK

GATHER

FOLD LINE

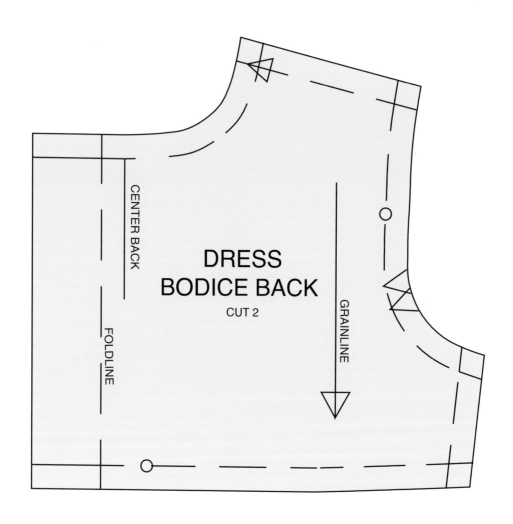

DRESS
BODICE BACK

CUT 2

CENTER BACK

FOLDLINE

GRAINLINE

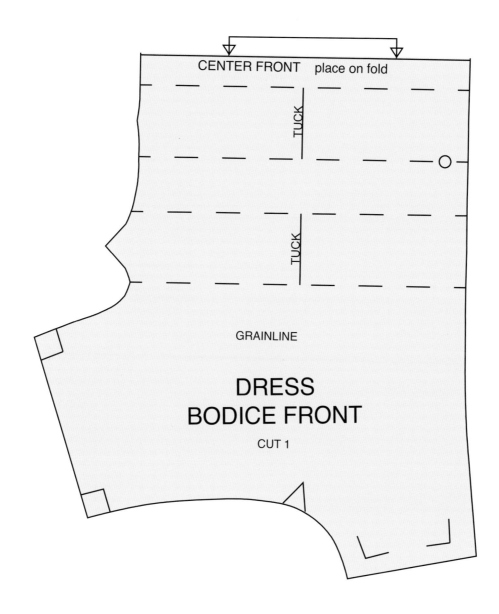

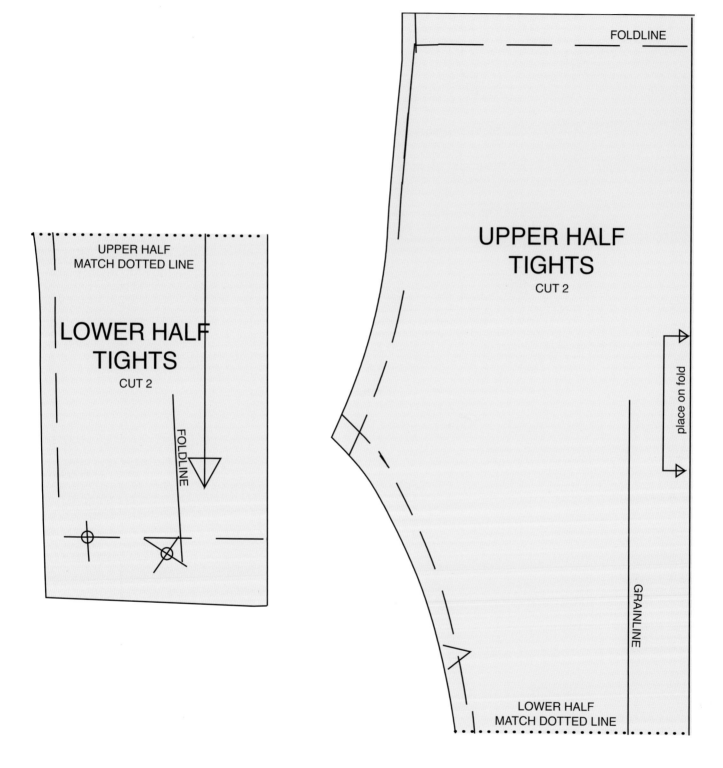

UPPER HALF
MATCH DOTTED LINE

LOWER HALF
TIGHTS

CUT 2

FOLDLINE

FOLDLINE

UPPER HALF
TIGHTS

CUT 2

place on fold

GRAINLINE

LOWER HALF
MATCH DOTTED LINE

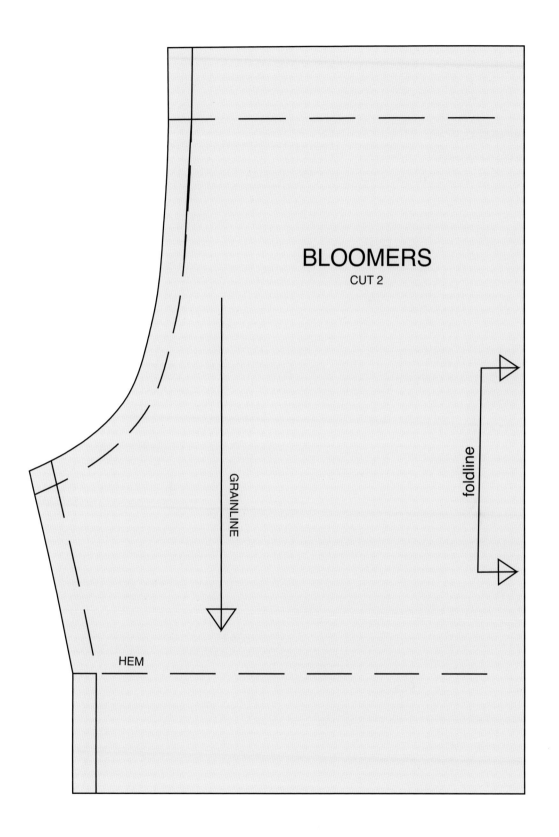

BLOOMERS

CUT 2

GRAINLINE

foldline

HEM

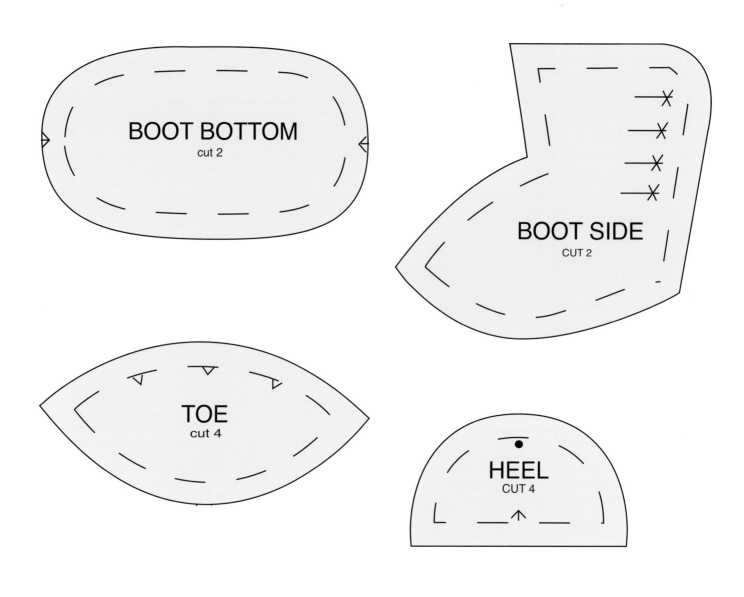

BOOT BOTTOM
cut 2

BOOT SIDE
CUT 2

TOE
cut 4

HEEL
CUT 4

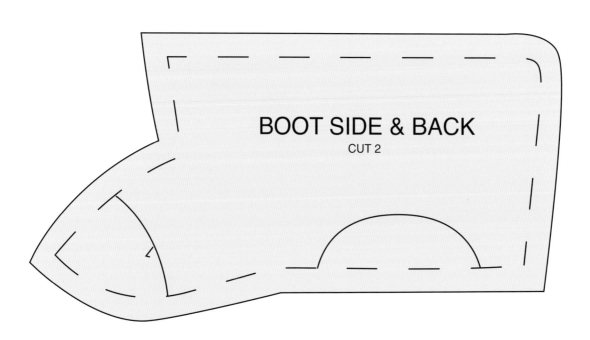

BOOT SIDE & BACK
CUT 2

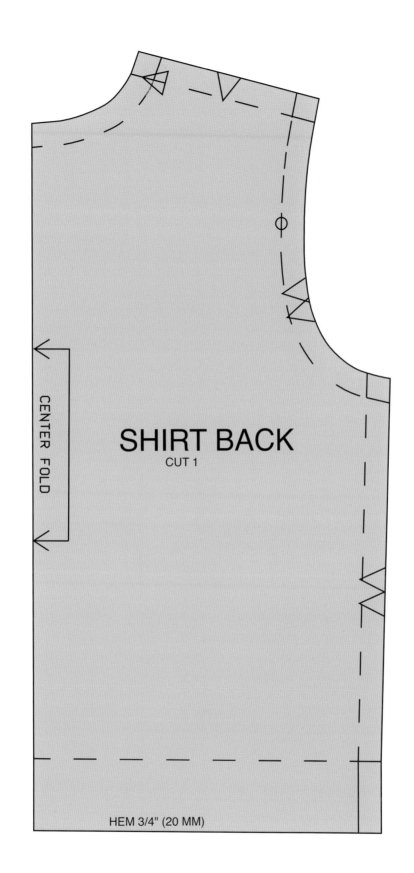

SHIRT BACK

CUT 1

CENTER FOLD

HEM 3/4" (20 MM)

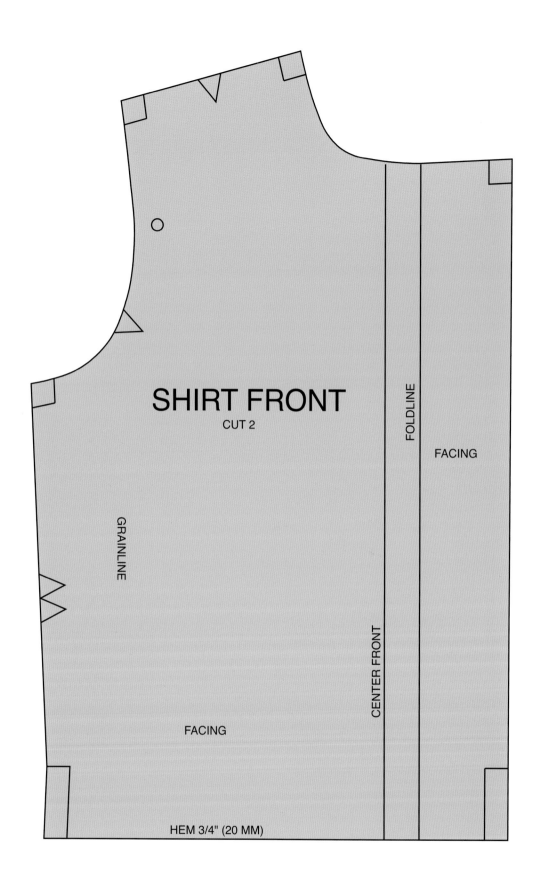

SHIRT FRONT

CUT 2

GRAINLINE

FOLDLINE

FACING

CENTER FRONT

FACING

HEM 3/4" (20 MM)

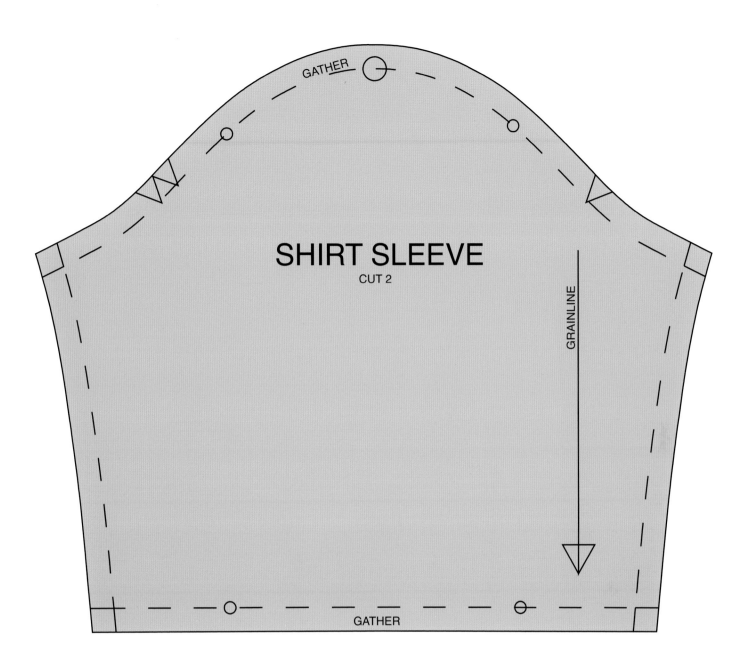

SHIRT SLEEVE

CUT 2

GATHER

GRAINLINE

GATHER

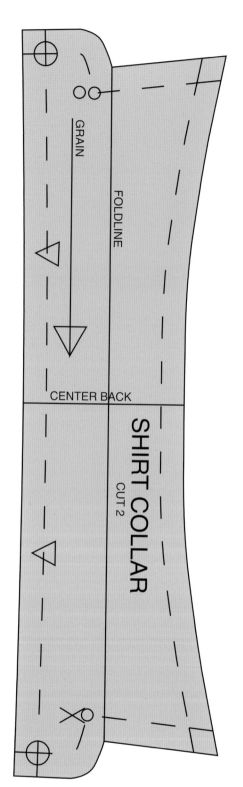

GRAIN

FOLDLINE

CENTER BACK

SHIRT COLLAR
CUT 2

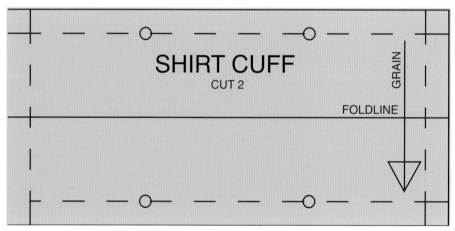

SHIRT CUFF
CUT 2

GRAIN

FOLDLINE

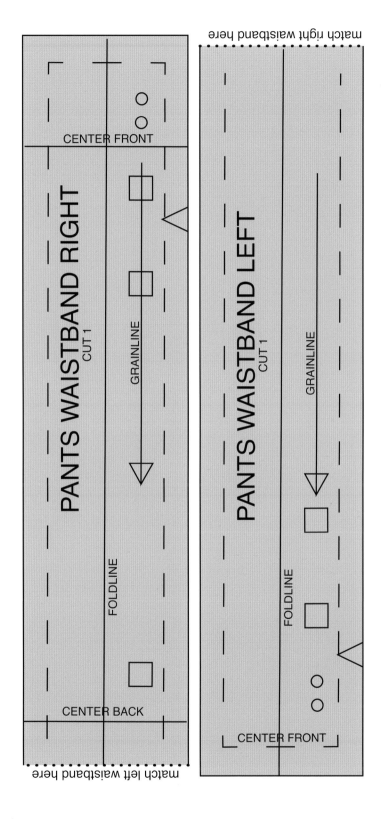

PANTS WAISTBAND RIGHT
CUT 1

CENTER FRONT

GRAINLINE

FOLDLINE

CENTER BACK

match left waistband here

PANTS WAISTBAND LEFT
CUT 1

match right waistband here

GRAINLINE

FOLDLINE

CENTER FRONT

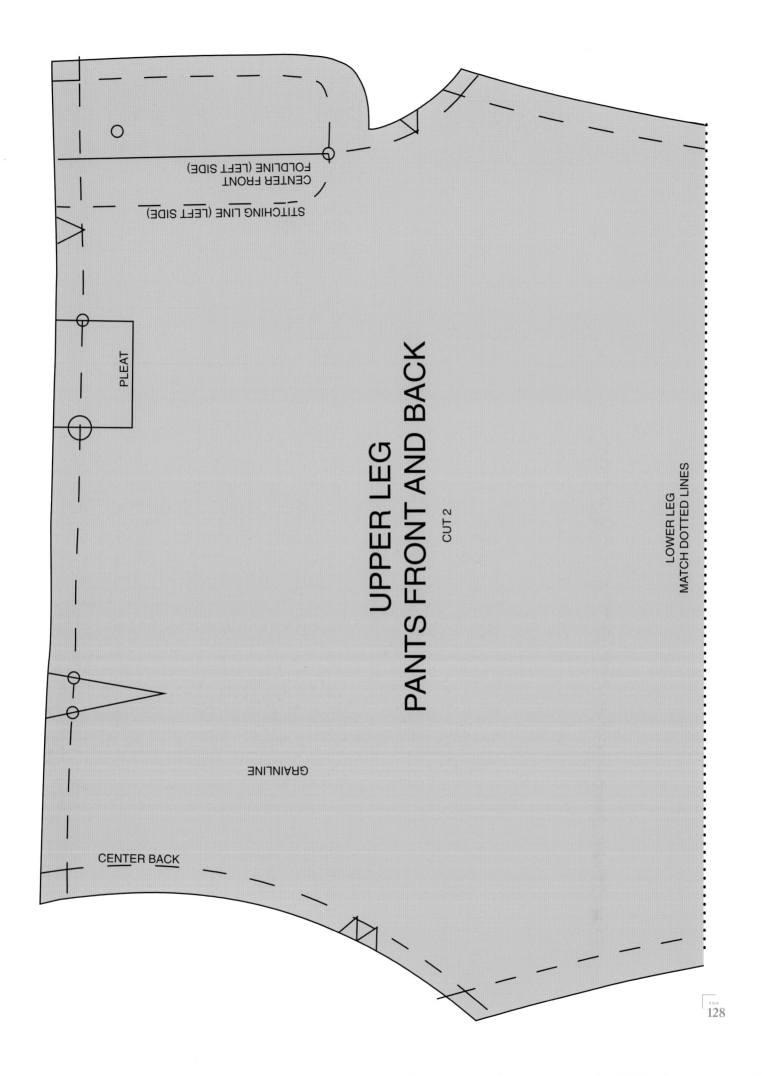

UPPER LEG
PANTS FRONT AND BACK

CUT 2

PLEAT

CENTER FRONT
FOLDLINE (LEFT SIDE)

STITCHING LINE (LEFT SIDE)

GRAINLINE

CENTER BACK

LOWER LEG
MATCH DOTTED LINES

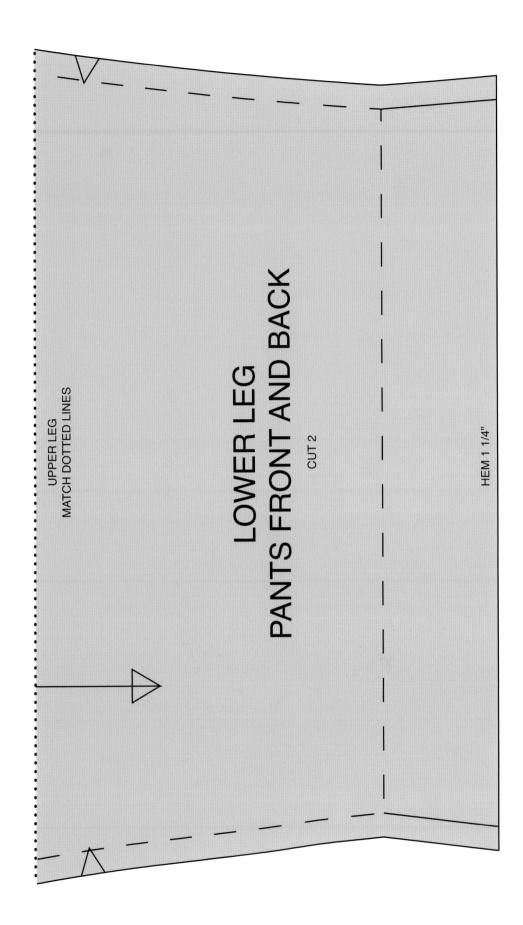

UPPER LEG
MATCH DOTTED LINES

LOWER LEG
PANTS FRONT AND BACK

CUT 2

HEM 1 1/4"

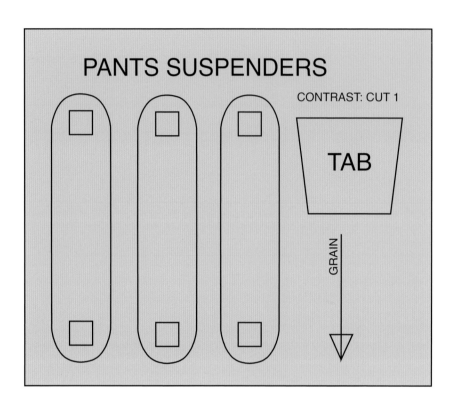

PANTS SUSPENDERS

CONTRAST: CUT 1

TAB

GRAIN

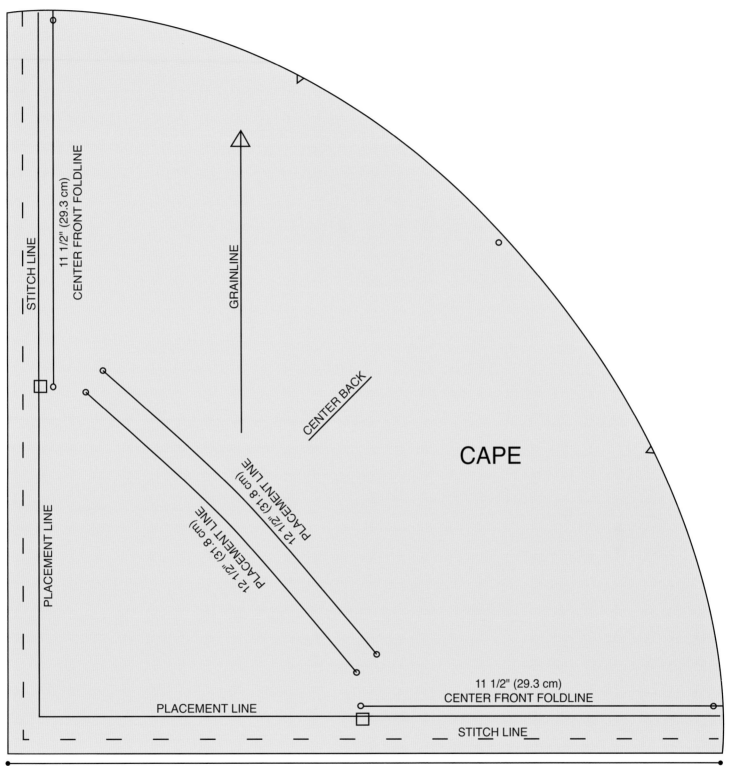

STITCH LINE

11 1/2" (29.3 cm)
CENTER FRONT FOLDLINE

GRAINLINE

PLACEMENT LINE

CENTER BACK

CAPE

12 1/2" (31.8 cm)
PLACEMENT LINE

12 1/2" (31.8 cm)
PLACEMENT LINE

11 1/2" (29.3 cm)
CENTER FRONT FOLDLINE

PLACEMENT LINE

STITCH LINE

23" (58.5 cm)

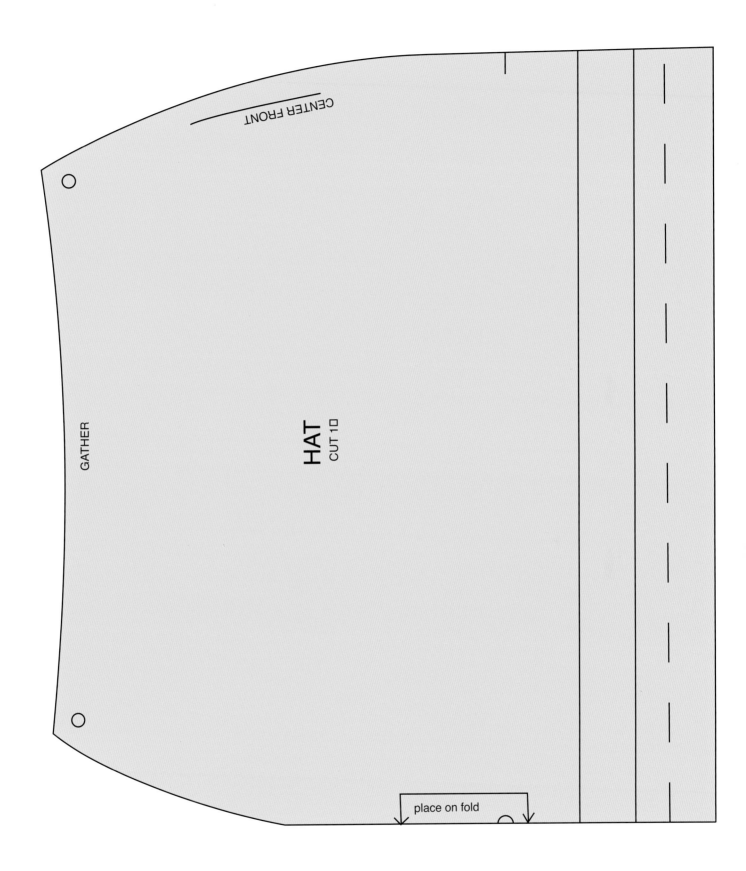

CENTER FRONT

GATHER

HAT
CUT 1

place on fold

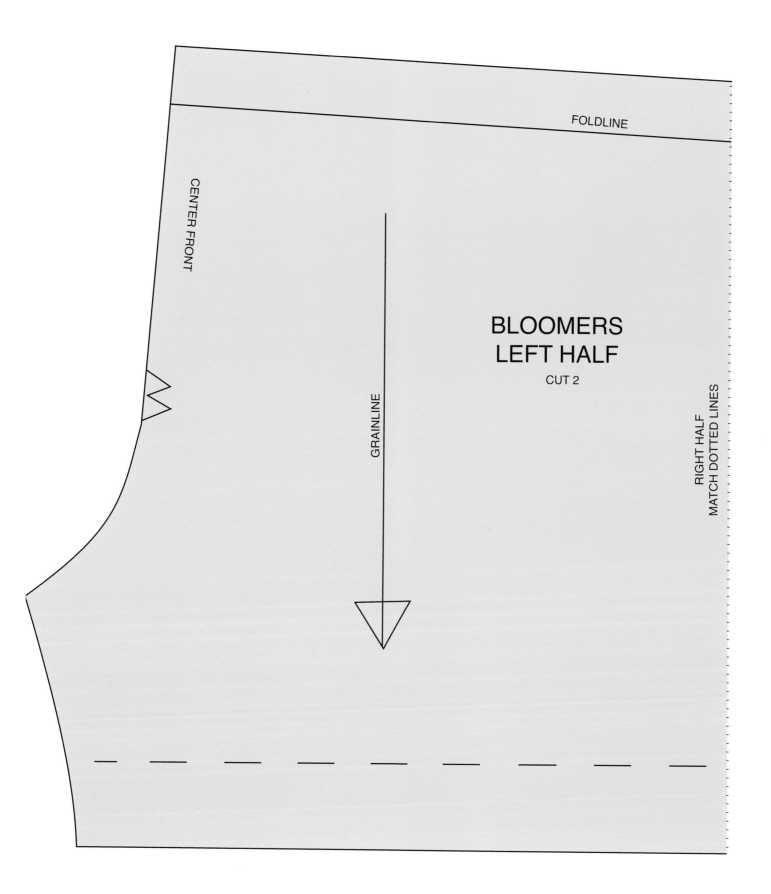

FOLDLINE

CENTER FRONT

GRAINLINE

**BLOOMERS
LEFT HALF**

CUT 2

RIGHT HALF
MATCH DOTTED LINES

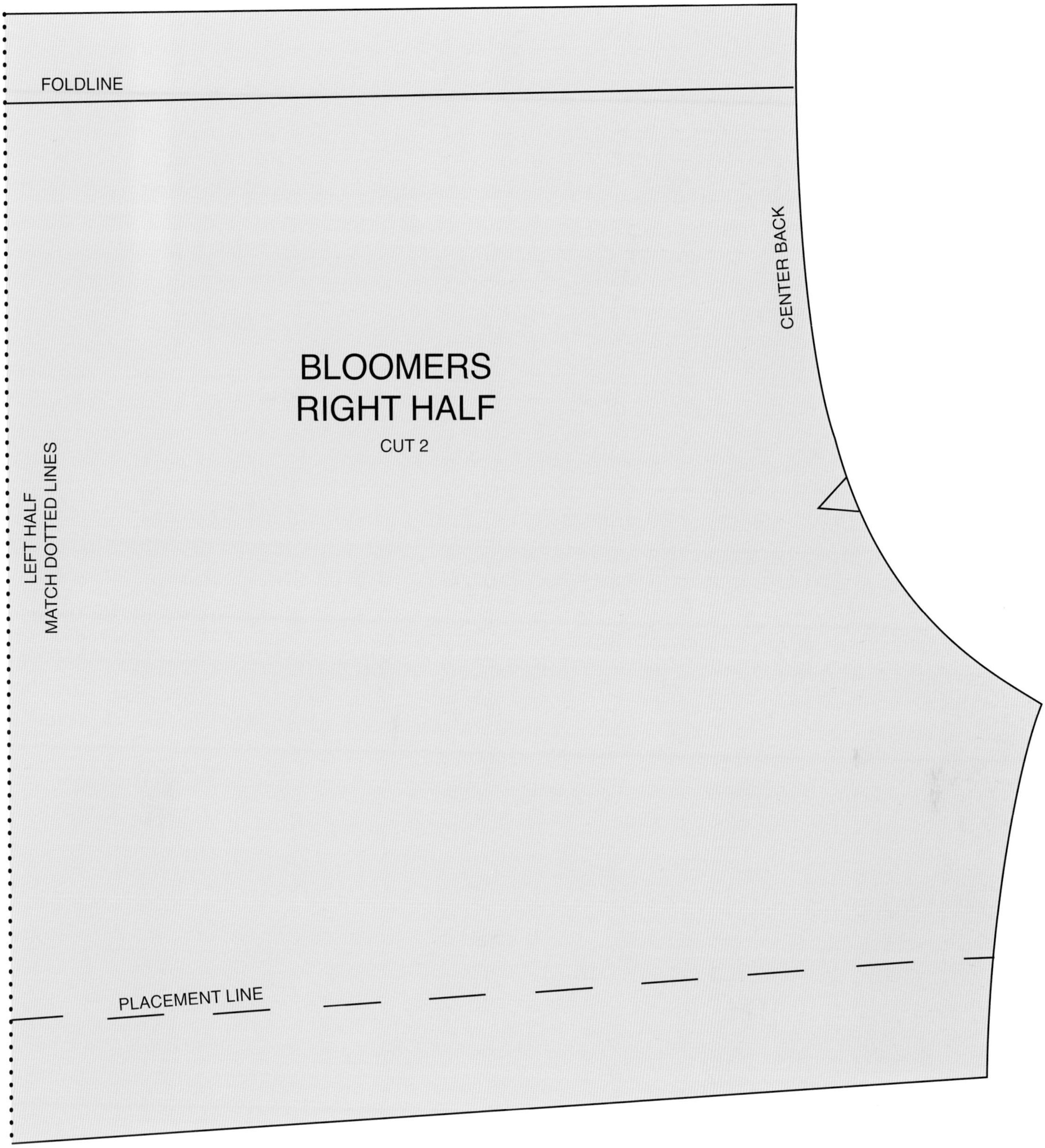

FOLDLINE

CENTER BACK

BLOOMERS
RIGHT HALF
CUT 2

LEFT HALF
MATCH DOTTED LINES

PLACEMENT LINE

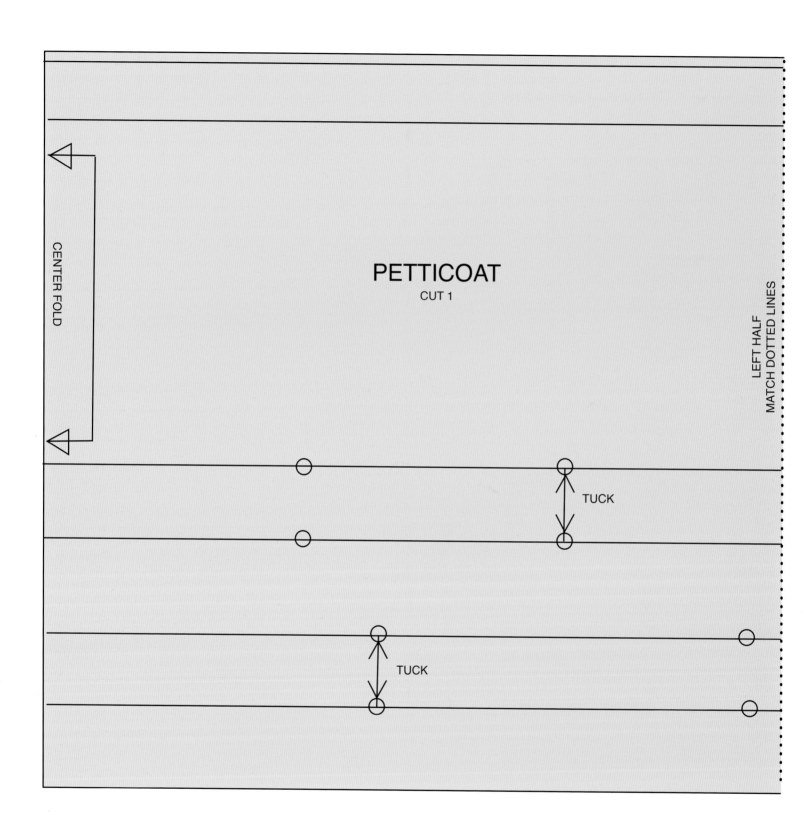

PETTICOAT

CUT 1

CENTER FOLD

LEFT HALF
MATCH DOTTED LINES

TUCK

TUCK

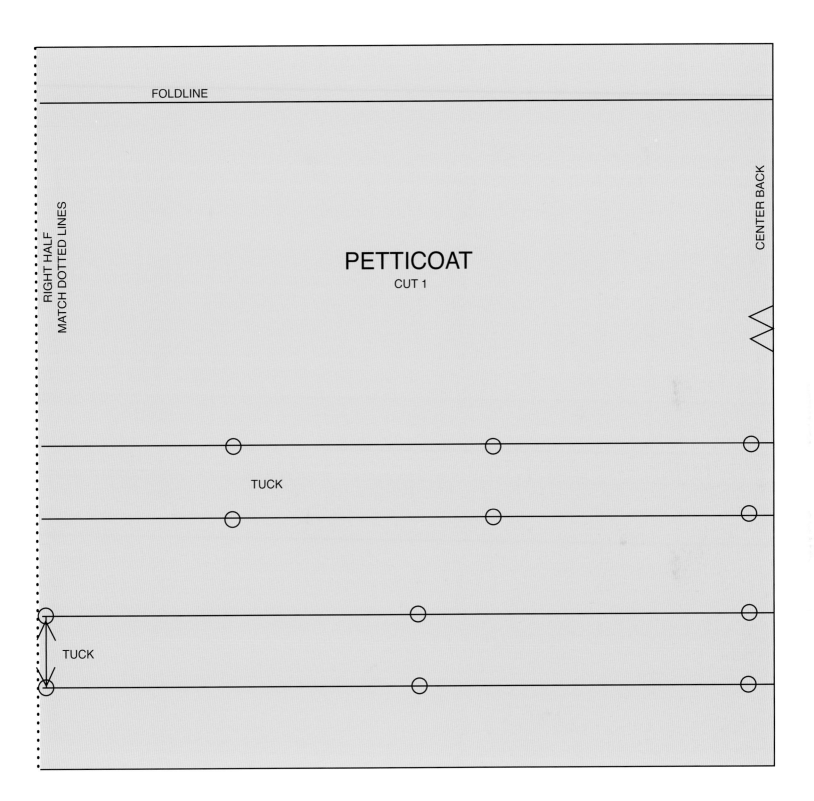

FOLDLINE

RIGHT HALF
MATCH DOTTED LINES

CENTER BACK

PETTICOAT
CUT 1

TUCK

TUCK

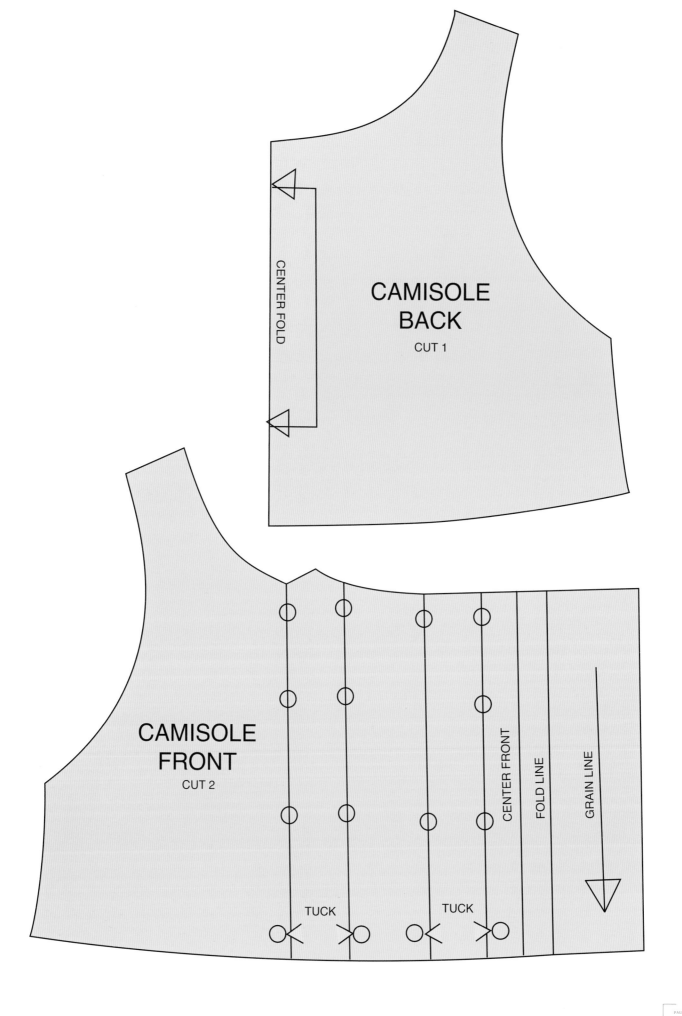

CAMISOLE
BACK

CUT 1

CENTER FOLD

CAMISOLE
FRONT

CUT 2

CENTER FRONT

FOLD LINE

GRAIN LINE

TUCK

TUCK

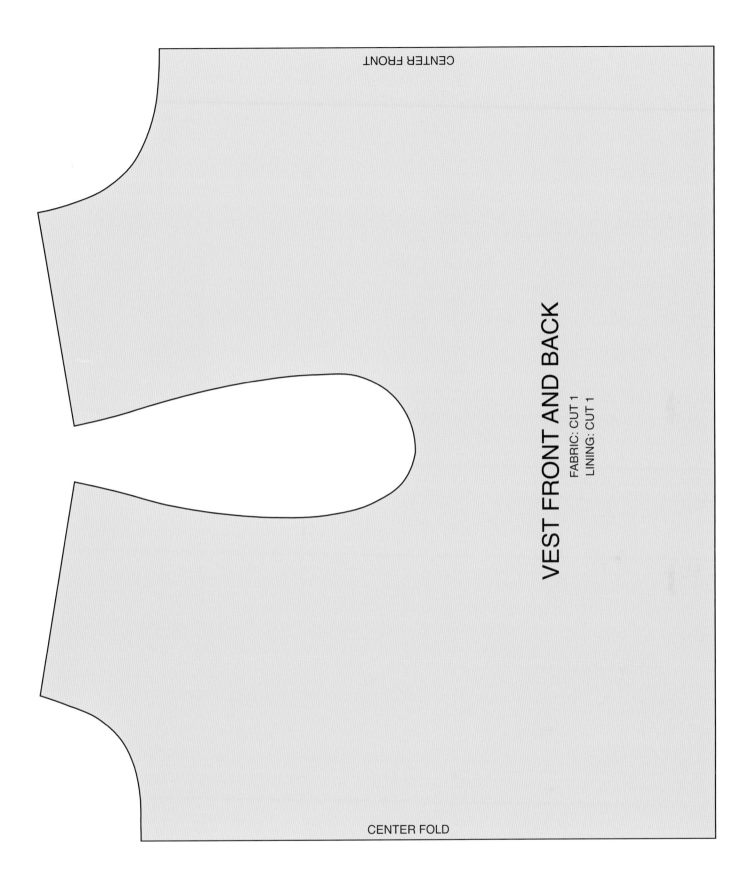

CENTER FRONT

VEST FRONT AND BACK

FABRIC: CUT 1
LINING: CUT 1

CENTER FRONT

CENTER FOLD

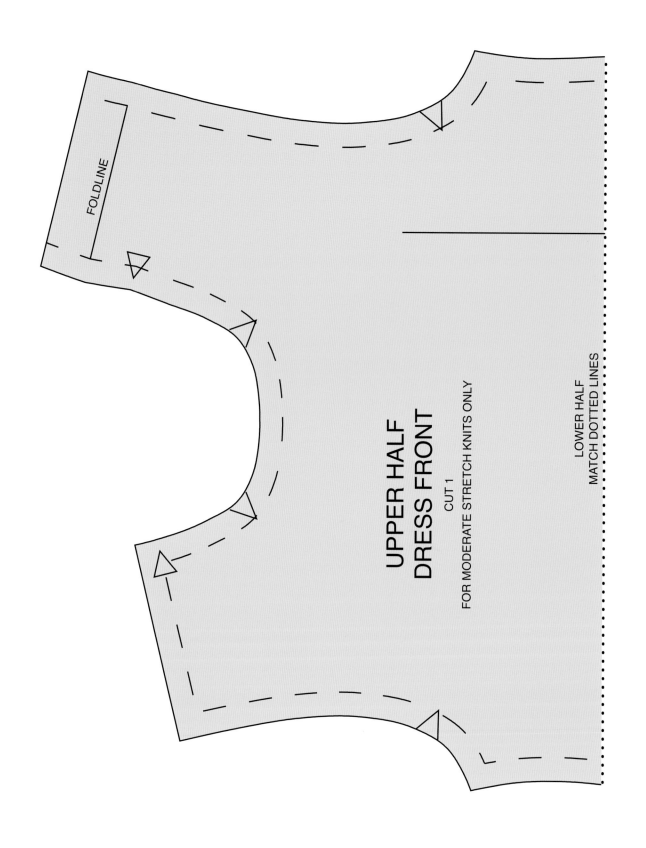

UPPER HALF
DRESS FRONT

CUT 1

FOR MODERATE STRETCH KNITS ONLY

FOLDLINE

LOWER HALF
MATCH DOTTED LINES

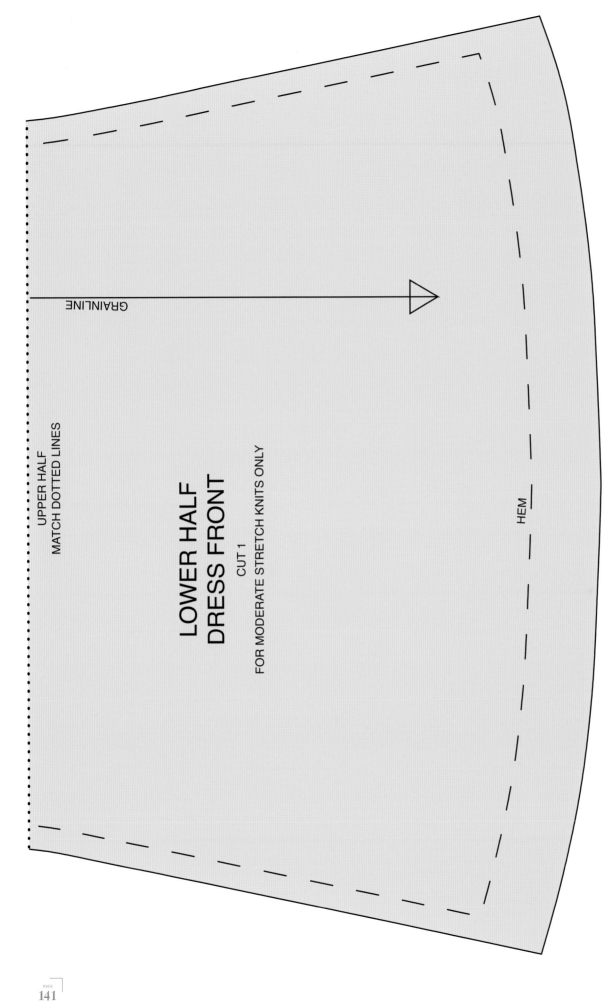

UPPER HALF
MATCH DOTTED LINES

LOWER HALF
DRESS FRONT

CUT 1

FOR MODERATE STRETCH KNITS ONLY

GRAINLINE

HEM

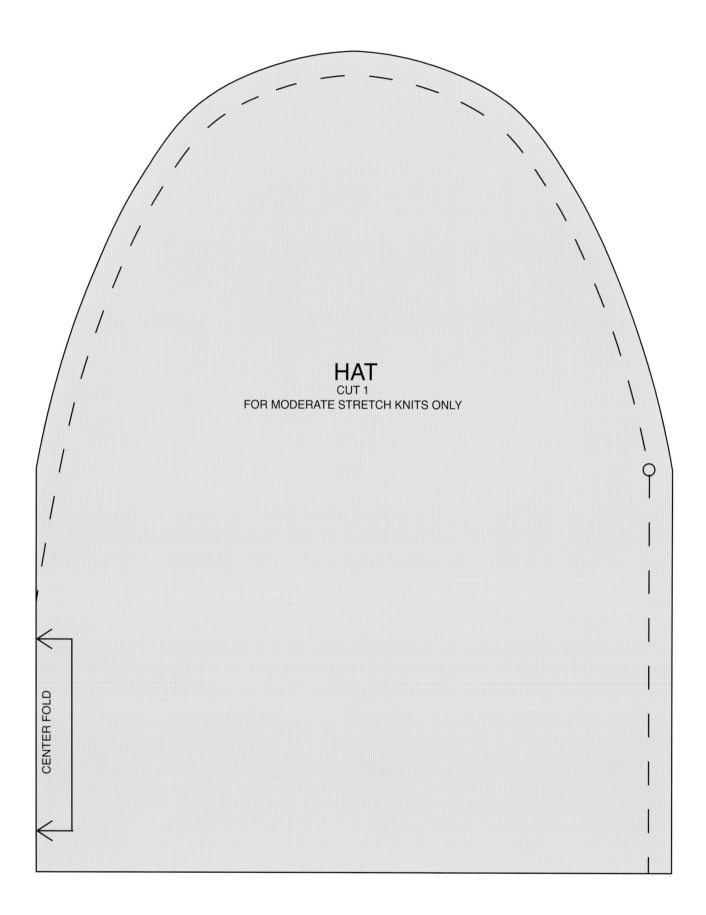

HAT
CUT 1
FOR MODERATE STRETCH KNITS ONLY

CENTER FOLD

DRESS SLEEVE

CUT 2

FOR MODERATE STRETCH KNITS ONLY

GRAINLINE

HEM

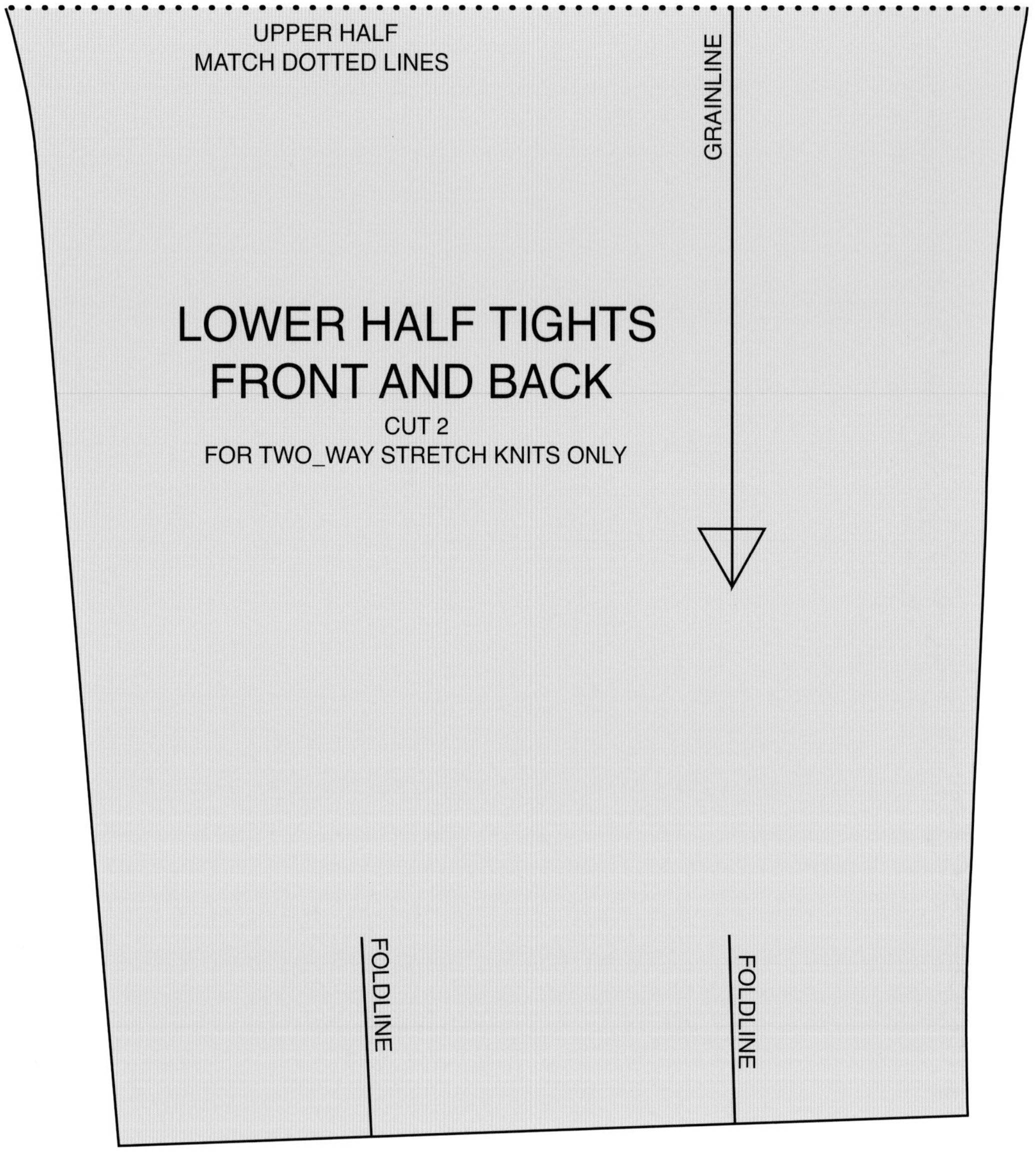

UPPER HALF
MATCH DOTTED LINES

GRAINLINE

LOWER HALF TIGHTS
FRONT AND BACK
CUT 2
FOR TWO_WAY STRETCH KNITS ONLY

FOLDLINE

FOLDLINE

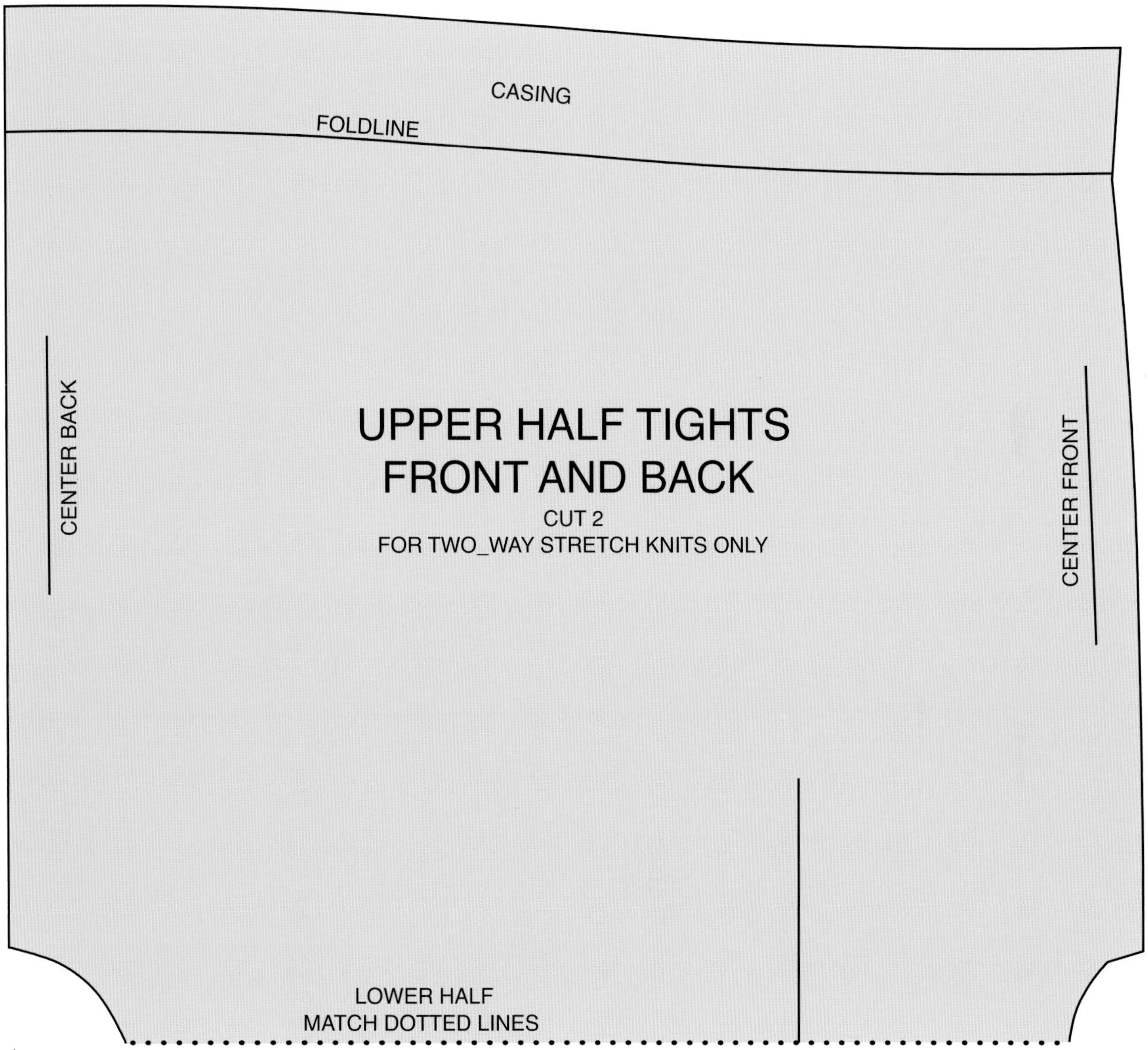

CASING

FOLDLINE

CENTER BACK

CENTER FRONT

UPPER HALF TIGHTS
FRONT AND BACK
CUT 2
FOR TWO_WAY STRETCH KNITS ONLY

LOWER HALF
MATCH DOTTED LINES

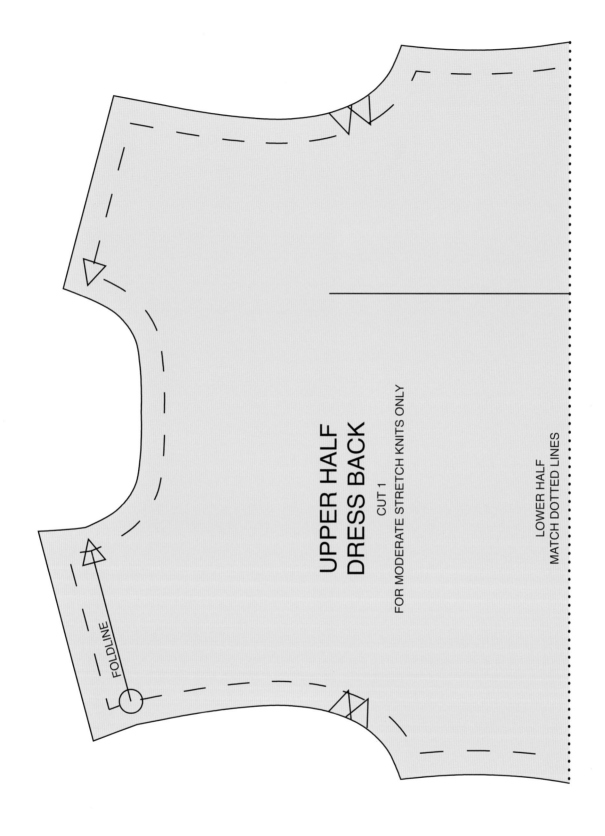

UPPER HALF
DRESS BACK

CUT 1

FOR MODERATE STRETCH KNITS ONLY

LOWER HALF
MATCH DOTTED LINES

FOLDLINE

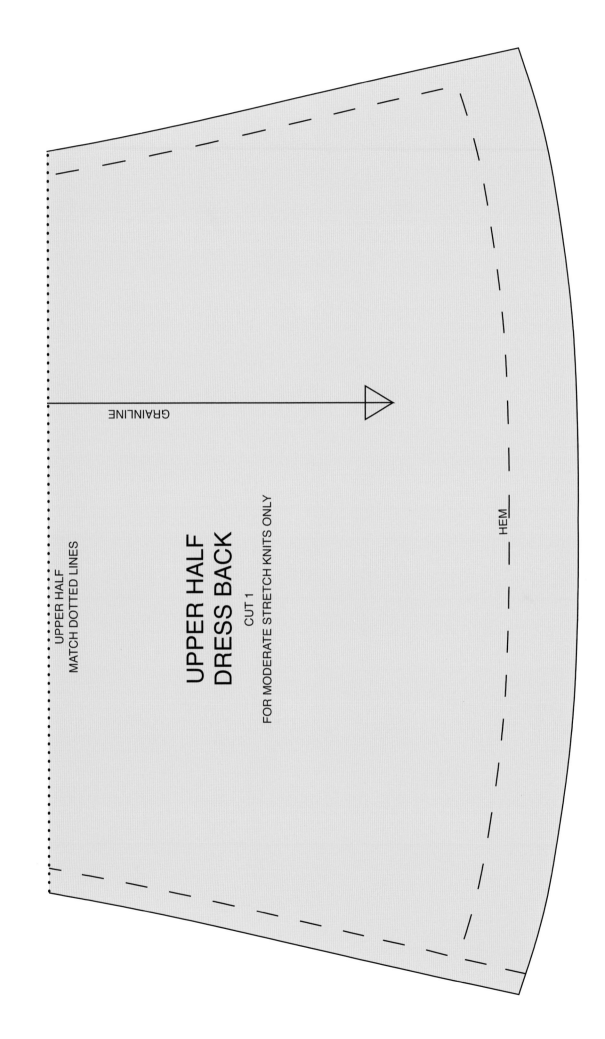

UPPER HALF
MATCH DOTTED LINES

UPPER HALF
DRESS BACK

CUT 1

FOR MODERATE STRETCH KNITS ONLY

GRAINLINE

HEM

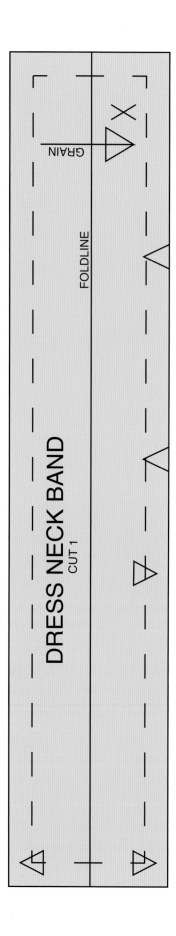

RIGHT RUFFLE
MATCH DOTTED LINE

LEFT
NIGHTSHIRT RUFFLE
CUT 1

CENTER FOLD

RIGHT RUFFLE
MATCH DOTTED LINE

CENTER BACK

HEM

RIGHT
NIGHTSHIRT RUFFLE
CUT 1

GATHER

LEFT RUFFLE
MATCH DOTTED LINE

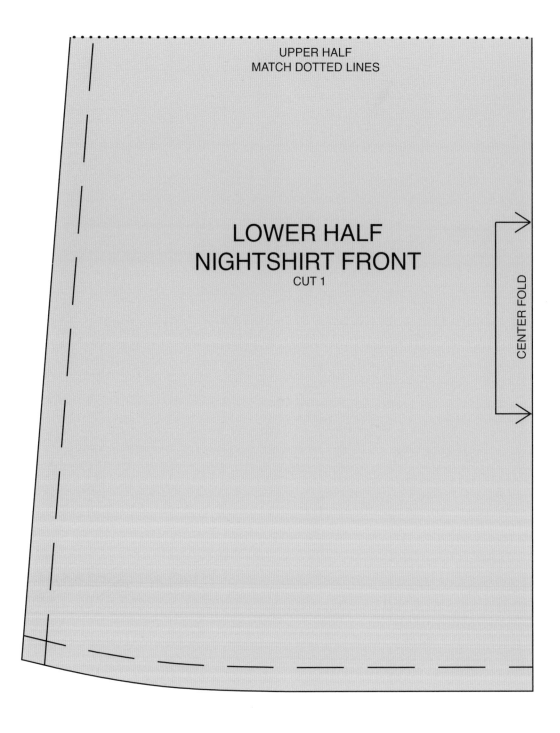

UPPER HALF
MATCH DOTTED LINES

LOWER HALF
NIGHTSHIRT FRONT
CUT 1

CENTER FOLD

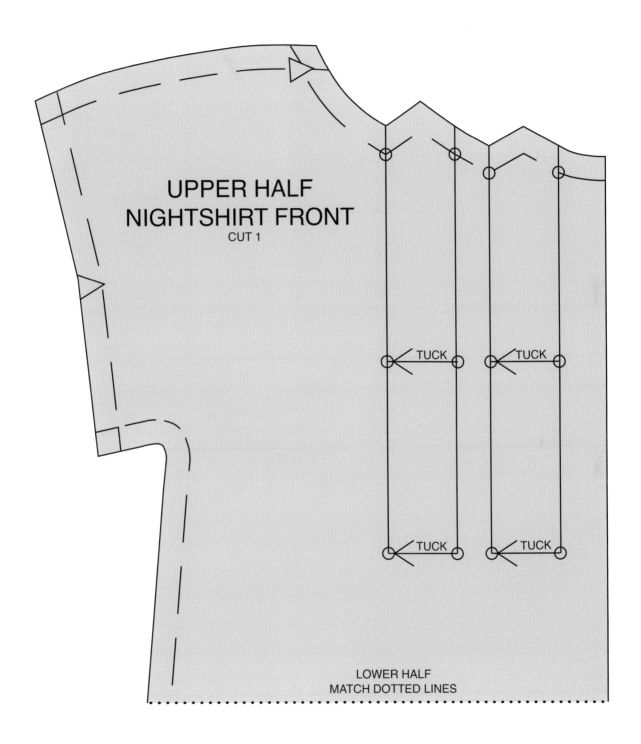

UPPER HALF
NIGHTSHIRT FRONT
CUT 1

TUCK

TUCK

TUCK

TUCK

LOWER HALF
MATCH DOTTED LINES

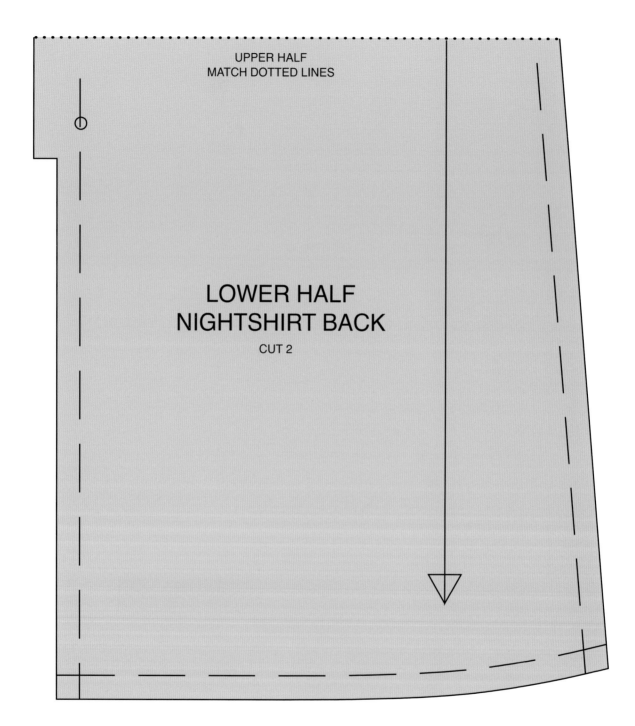

UPPER HALF
MATCH DOTTED LINES

LOWER HALF
NIGHTSHIRT BACK

CUT 2

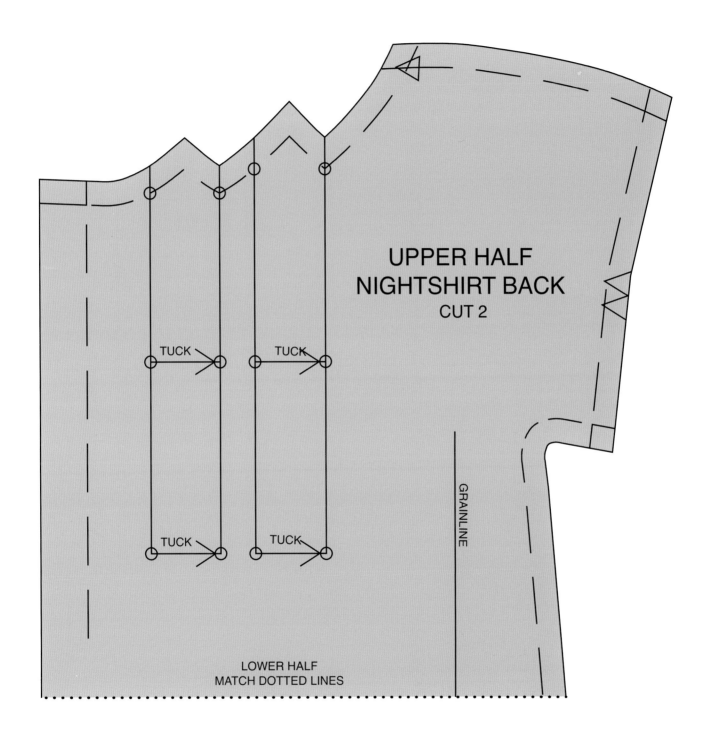

UPPER HALF
NIGHTSHIRT BACK
CUT 2

TUCK

TUCK

TUCK

TUCK

GRAINLINE

LOWER HALF
MATCH DOTTED LINES

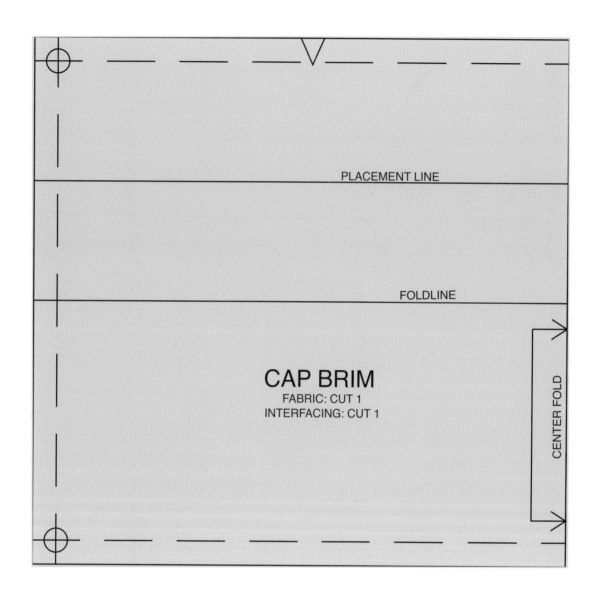

PLACEMENT LINE

FOLDLINE

CAP BRIM
FABRIC: CUT 1
INTERFACING: CUT 1

CENTER FOLD

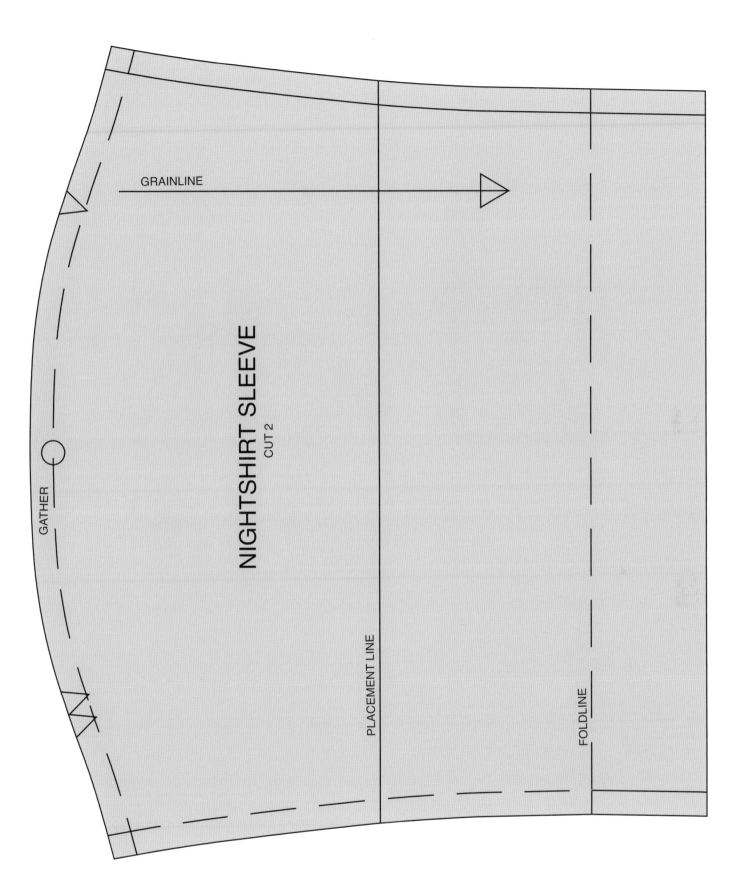

GRAINLINE

GATHER

NIGHTSHIRT SLEEVE
CUT 2

PLACEMENT LINE

FOLDLINE

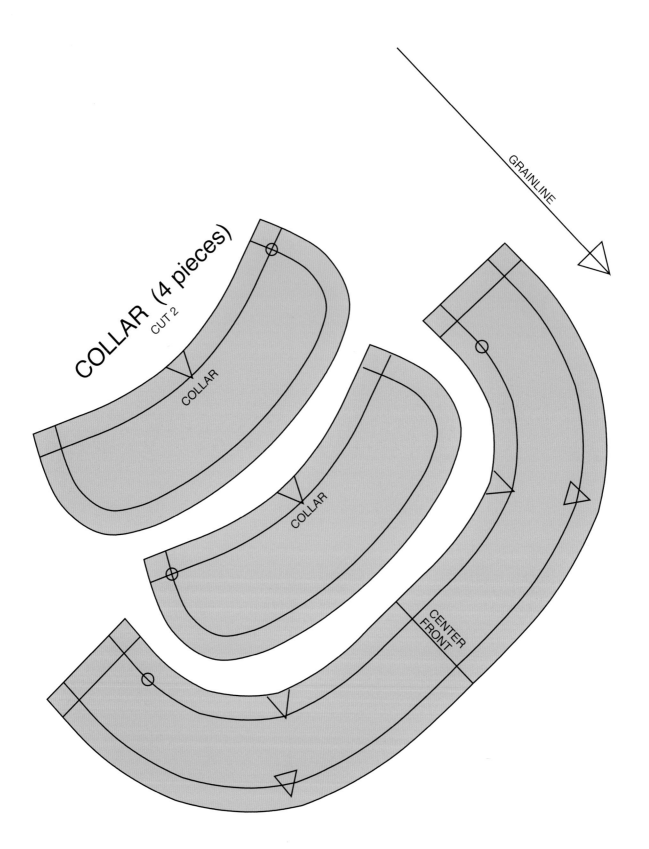

COLLAR (4 pieces)
CUT 2

COLLAR

COLLAR

CENTER FRONT

GRAINLINE

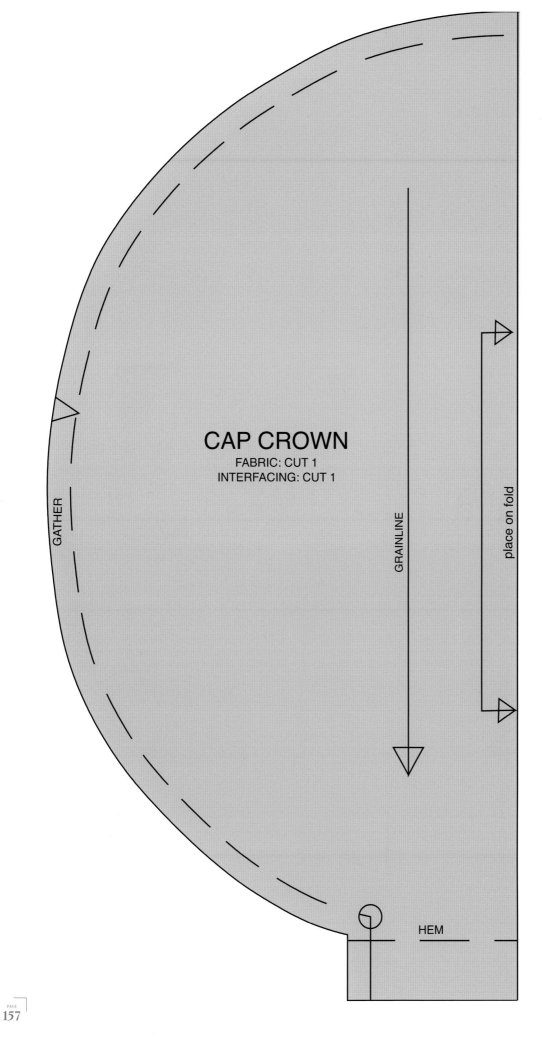

CAP CROWN

FABRIC: CUT 1
INTERFACING: CUT 1

GATHER

GRAINLINE

place on fold

HEM

Resource List

FABRICS:

Banksville Designer Fabrics
115 New Canaan Avenue (Rt. 123)
Norwalk, CT 06850
203-846-1333
www.banksville@juno.com

Fabric Center
484 Electric Avenue
P.O. Box 8212
Fitchburg, MA 01420
508-343-4403
FAX 508-343-8139

Fabrics.com
814 E. Livingston CT
Marietta, GA 30067
888-455-2940
www.fabric.com

N.Y. Theatrical Supply, Inc.
263 W. 38th St., Store #3
New York, NY 10018
212-840-3120
FAX 212-840-3159

DOLL WIGS:

Dollsparts
99 Gold St.
Brooklyn, NY 11201
1-800-336-DOLL (3655)
www.dollspartsupply@aol.com

YARNS:

Black Sheep Wools
P.O. Box 9205
Lowell, MA 01855
508-937-0320
FAX 508-452-3085

The Fiber Studio
9 Foster Hill Rd.
P.O. Box 637CSS
Henniker, NH 03242
603-428-7830

Ironstone Warehouse
P.O. Box 365
Lixbridge, MA 01569
Orders: 800-343-4914
Information: 508-278-5838
FAX 508-278-7433

Northeast Knitworks
P.O. Box 109
Freeport, ME 04032
207-865-3412
FAX 207-865-3418

NOTIONS & TRIMS

Atlantic Thread Co.
695 Red Oak Road
Stockbridge, GA 30281
800-847-1001
FAX 800-298-0403

Clotilde Inc.
B3000
Louisiana, MO 63353-3000
800-545-4002
www.clotilde.com

Ginsco Trims
242 W. 38th St. Dept. TR
New York, NY 10018
800-929-2529
www.ginstrim.com

Greensberg & Hammer
24 W. 57th St.
New York, NY 10019
800-955-5135
FAX 212-765-8475

**Hyman Hendler
& Sons**
67 W. 38th St.
New York, NY 10018
212-840-8393

Mokuba NY
55 West 39th Street
New York, NY 10018
212-869-8900

Nancy's Notions
P.O. Box 683 Dept. 32
Beaver Dam, WI 53916
414-887-0891
FAX 414-887-2133
www.nancysnotions.com

Tinsel Trading Co.
47 West 38th St.
New York, NY 10018
212-730-1030
FAX 212-768-8823

Acknowledgments

I wish to express my thanks and gratitude to all of the people who have made this book possible.

First and foremost, to my husband Jon for his years of endless encouragement and love, and to my children, Rachel and Jonathan, who continue to be constant sources of inspiration. And to my mother, who taught me how to sew at the age of twelve.

To the people at Vogue® Craft Patterns for many wonderful years of working together. With special thanks to Joan Watkins and Joe Anselmo who gave me the opportunity and freedom to design without restrictions.

Thanks to the great team at SoHo Publishing, whose efforts made this book possible, including Trisha Malcom, Beth Baumgartel, Annemarie McNamara, Ben Ostasiewski and the photography of Brian Kraus.

To my most valued assistant, Ann Baldwin for her patience and caring.

Last, but not least, to Madeline, my cat, who is my constant companion in the sewing room.